Love Through the Eyes

of a Sixteen Year Old

Author

Anonymous

Love Through The Eyes of a Sixteen Year Old

The characters and the story in this book are fiction.

www.chelseasongbird.com

Printed in the United States of America

All Rights Reserved

Library of Congress Control Number: 2010914037

ISBN 978-0-9846217-1-2

Introduction

    This book is about a sixteen year old who has her first crush on a boy named Jeff. The young man she has a crush on has an accident caused by a faulty football helmet. He spends several months in a hospital and when he wakes up he hasn't a clue who Chelsea Songbird is. He doesn't even remember how to tie his shoelaces. Chelsea has gone through the year under a dark cloud because of Jeff's condition, but the cloud is lifted when she joins a summer soccer team that brought the sunshine back into her life. Soccer gave Chelsea a happy love for life once again.

Acknowledgments

This book was as much of a joy to write as my first book, Love Through the Eyes of a Fifteen Year Old. The characters are a year older and are wise beyond their years. I want to acknowledge all sixteen-year-olds who can relate to this book. Enjoy your read.

www.chelseasongbird.com

Table of Contents

Chapter 1
Cloie's Return

My summer vacation in Pensacola, Florida, was a blast. Being able to have my own hotel room next to my parents made me feel so mature. That was the whole point of having my own room; to become more mature and responsible for my actions. My parents planned it that way.

Summer vacation is coming to an end and soon I will be back in school with my friends. Right now I'm taking a summer course in Driver's Ed so I can pass my driver's test when I turn sixteen. I have a great teacher who started me out on back roads with little to no traffic. I don't know if this was for his safety or mine. Either way, it was very comfortable driving with no traffic while I was getting to know my instructor. By the way, his name is Ed. By taking this course, my car insurance will cost less. My parents are very thrifty and believe that teaching me the economical way to do things is their duty as parents. Their motto is, "Never throw money away and always look for ways to save a dollar, because someday you might need those dollars." It makes a lot of sense, seeing how insurance is higher for sports cars than it is for just a regular family car. You see, I will be driving a Mustang when I get my driver's license. I don't plan on hot rodding, but I've always liked the look of a Mustang.

I turn 16 on July 25th and plan to take my driving test that morning. Ed seems to think I will be ready by then. Today we are driving in traffic and I am not having any problems. I just kind of go with the flow of the traffic and occasionally check my speedometer to be sure I am not going over the speed limit. Going over the speed limit and forgetting to give turn signals seem to be Ed's pet peeves.

I'm glad I live in a small town where there is not a lot of traffic because today Ed wants me to try to parallel park. This is the hardest part of the driving test. Ed informed me that I should take a deep breath and take my time. No need to get in a hurry. The first time I turned my wheels to start backing into the parking space, Ed immediately stopped me. He told me if I continued at the angle I was turning the wheel, I would scrape the side of the car. Ed had me pull back up beside the parked car again. Then as I started to back into the parking space again, he told me to cut my wheels harder to the right as I backed into the parking space and then back to the left after I was past the bumper of the parked car. With Ed's patience and ability to keep me calm, I had mastered parallel parking by the end of the day.

Ed released me from Driver's Ed and wished me good luck on my test. I shook his hand and thanked him for being so patient with me.

My sister Cloie has been overseas as a foreign exchange student in France and is coming home for my birthday. My parents always celebrate our birthdays. After all, it was a big day for them when we were born. My mom always likes to remind us of the exact time we were born. I was born at 2:16 in the morning and Cloie was born at 5:47 in the morning. Mom says that most people only know what day and year they were born, but with us, it's a family tradition to know the hour of your birth as well.

Cloie missed going on vacation with us, but no way would she miss my birthday. Sixteen is considered a very special milestone in our house. When Cloie turned sixteen, she got her Driver's License that morning, and a Jeep that afternoon. Cloie took all of us driving around for two hours in her birthday present. It was a fine day. I hope to repeat this day in my Mustang, if I pass my Driver's Test that is.

Cloie's airplane is scheduled to arrive at 2:30 p.m. today. I haven't seen her in over a year and I'm so excited that I can't even put it into words. We have always been very close and have keep in contact but it's just not the same as having her back in the house with us. I just want to give her a big hug.

Dad washed the car this morning, filled the gas tank, and picked up some fresh fruit for breakfast. We were all going into town to pick up my sister. It is around a four-hour drive from our home in Tahlequah to Oklahoma City. We had a great time singing songs and telling stories on our way to the airport. Cloie seemed to be the main topic of our conversation. Mom talked about the time Cloie got lost in the Wildlife Refuge behind our house. She was going horseback riding when a bobcat jumped out and startled her horse. The horse ran for at least three miles before Cloie could get control of it. That may not sound like a long distance, but for a ten-year-old girl, it's a world away from home.

Cloie told us that when the horse finally came to a stop, she looked around to see where she was and did not recognize a single thing. The horse had gotten off the beaten path and had plowed through brush that hadn't been disturbed in years. Cloie was surprised that even a horse was able to plow through the thick brush. When she dismounted the horse she noticed blood was dripping from the chest of the horse. The brush had apparently ripped the flesh from the horse's chest and front legs. Cloie gathered some large leaves and loose dirt and packed them into the open wounds. All she could think about was stopping the bleeding.

Once the horse settled down and all the patchwork was in place, Cloie realized she better figure out how to find her way back through the blackberry bushes that had injured the horse. No, she decided, that would not be the way to go. She would have to go around these bushes. But first, she needed a landmark to take her back to the direction from which she came. She noticed a dark green pine that stood out from all the other trees. She would use this tree as her landmark after she had circled the bushes. Cloie did not dare mount the horse for two reasons. First of all, because the horse was injured, and second because if the horse got spooked again for some reason, it would probably take her even further away from home.

Cloie began leading the horse around the brush by its reins, while keeping an eye on the tree she was using as a landmark. When she finally made it to the tree, which seemed like it took forever, she was faced with the dilemma of where she was to go from there. It was time for a break so she tied the horse to a tree and sat on the ground. As she looked all around for a sign that would point her in the right direction, she came to the conclusion that she was in a predicament that was defying a satisfactory solution. She then cleared her head and began to pray to God. This always calms her down so that she can make good decisions. Her heart was heavy with melancholy feelings when suddenly she noticed a hoof print from her horse. Like a little ray of sunshine, that hoof print made her heart burst with joy as she realized all she had to do was follow the tracks her horse had laid out for her on the way there.

Dad told us that God showed Cloie the tracks and her Native American Cherokee heritage showed her how to follow them. I am sure Cloie would be in complete agreement with this statement. By the time Cloie had made it back to the house, she was exhausted. She poured herself a large glass of ice tea, told her story to her parents, and asked if they would call the vet for the horse.

The veterinarian patched up Cloie's horse with some stitches and antibiotics. An antibiotic is a substance that is produced by organisms such as fungi and bacteria, effective in the suppression or destruction of microorganisms, and widely used in the prevention and treatment of diseases. Because Cloie used dirt to stop the bleeding, her horse could get a severe infection caused from microorganism in the dirt. The vet instructed Cloie to use oral and topical antibiotics for ten days.

Her horse got well and lived another five years. Cloie sold her horse to a processing plant when it broke its leg. It was the kind of break that would never heal. The horse would be in constant pain if allowed to live. It may sound cold-hearted to sell a pet to a processing plant, but Cloie wanted to see something good come out of the death of her horse. This horse would become food for somebody, or for some dogs. You see, in France, horse is considered a delicacy, which is something pleasing and appealing to have for dinner. Horse is a very lean meat and is quite healthy. In the United States it is illegal to process a horse for human consumption. The last horse killed for dog food in the United States was September 21, 2007. At the present time there are no more plants operating that process horse in the U.S.

I wonder what people do with their horses if they need to be put down. It sounds like another bad law. Some special interest group paid their way into taking that right away from country folk.

Cloie's motto has always been, if some good can come from your actions, it is selfish to not act on it. A good example of this is that everyone in our family are organ donors. If we can help someone with our donation it is a selfless act. On the other hand, being concerned only or primarily with oneself without regard for others is selfish. Lawmakers need to look at this law and reconsider what they have done. They are guilty of wastefulness. Bad laws should be taken off the books.

Dad is now pulling into the parking lot of the airport. We are all so excited about seeing Cloie. We are only a few minutes early, so we were in a rush to beat her airplane.

As we were quickly walking, Dad said, "Let's not tell Cloie about that fish that punctured my leg on vacation or that hog that scared Chelsea under the apple tree yet. We don't want Cloie to worry about us while she is so far from home. After all she will only be here for a week. Let's keep the mood light."

As we entered the airport, Dad stopped to check the flight schedule board, he said, "We can relax. We still have ten minutes before touchdown, so let's slow it down and catch our breath." Dad still had problems walking fast since that fish punctured his leg on vacation. The doctor told him it would be six months before he was 100% recovered. If he is just walking you can't tell there is a problem, but running is difficult for him.

I was the first to see Cloie after her plane landed and ran to give her a hug.

She grabbed me and said, "Chelsea, you look great! You are so grown up. I missed you!"

I told her that I had missed her too and was so glad that she was finally here. Dad was next in line and Cloie grabbed him for a hug.

Dad said, "Welcome home, my little Indian princess."

Cloie answered, "It is so good to hear your voice! Come here, Mom, I want to hug both of you at the same time!"

Mom answered, "Daughter, I am so glad you are home! I've missed you. Did you have a good flight?"

Cloie replied, "I missed you, Mom, and it was a long

flight! I had to change airplanes twice! I am just glad to be home for seven days."

After saying our hellos we headed for the car.

Dad asked, "Is anybody hungry?"

We all answered with a big, "Yes!" Whenever we come to the city we always go to this all-you-can-eat restaurant. This way everyone gets what they want to eat and all they want. Mom and Dad always get fish, I get chicken and Cloie gets beef.

The main topic of conversation was food in France. Cloie started off talking about the wonderful breads they have that are always fresh-baked. Breads with the French are always a main part of every meal. Cloie's favorite is the long, thin, crusty baguette. Cloie said, "The French never cut their baguettes, they just break them off in chunks." Fresh baked bread with every meal sounds delightful to me. It is one of my favorite foods.

Cloie talked about how all kinds of meat are popular in France. Beef, horse, chicken, pork, rabbit, lamb, and various types of games, which are served with rich sauces. Most of the sauces have wine in them. The country makes a quarter of all the world's wine, and no main course is complete without a taste of it. There are over 400 different kinds of cheeses in France. Food is a passion of the French people and the afternoon meal could often last as long as two hours. It is the largest meal of the day. French cooks insist on the freshest of ingredients of the highest quality and shop carefully for the best value. Rating restaurants is a sport in the culinary world in France and the result of this competitiveness is a fabulous cuisine that has a great influence on the food of other lands.

I had to interrupt Cloie because she mentioned horse as one of the meats served in French restaurants. I said, "Cloie, my sweet sister, did you try the horse?"

Cloie responded, "As a matter of fact, I did. It is quite tasty, but a little bit chewy. Horsemeat is very lean and very good for building your red blood cells. I thought about my horse Buddy while I was eating my first serving. I thought about all the joy he had brought into my life while he was alive, and in death how he was able to nourish a body instead of feeding some low life worms in his grave. It is a shame we cannot serve horse in the USA because it is quite healthy for you and very low in fat. Speaking of fat, you seldom see an overweight Frenchman. They serve smaller portions and eat very slow so that they can fill up on less."

Mom changed the subject and asked, "How is your French coming along?"

Cloie replied, "I'm not fluent yet but I will be. Right now, I will give you a short lesson in French so you can see the beauty of the language. Monsieur means Mr. or Sir, and Madame means Mrs.. Mademoiselle mean Miss or young lady. It is not considered rude to use these titles without using the person's name. That comes in handy when you forget whom you are talking to, or you just don't know their name. The word bon voyage is a French word as well as café'. Language is so fascinating to study. It has a charm and elegance that only those who study it learn to appreciate. You know Dad, when you taught me to speak Cherokee you opened my eyes to the power that language could give a person. I thank you for that."

Dad smiled and said, "My pleasure. We should head for home so that we get there before dark."

We loaded up in the car and headed to Tahlequah, our home. On our way home Cloie talked about the French architecture, which is a mix of the mid-12th century Gothic style, which consists of pointed arches and colorful stained-glass, to the more modern architecture of the most famous museums in the world, like the Louvre. She talked about the Eiffel Tower and how she took a ride to the top for a breathtaking view of Paris. Her favorite however is a string of beautiful chateaus that stretch along the valley of the Loire

River. Here she saw Amboise, Chaumont, and Chenonceau, which are all castles that are several centuries old.

My favorite story was how she went snow skiing in the Alps. She talked about how many of the French spend their leisure time skiing in pursuit of physical fitness. I can relate to this because I love nature and I get my own physical fitness by playing basketball. I also liked hearing about the annual Tour de France bicycle race. Each July, around 200 professional racers from all over the world compete in this event. The cyclist who wins each day gets to wear a yellow vest so all will know that he was the best that day. Whoever wins overall always becomes a millionaire through endorsements and advertising.

Another of my favorite stories she told was about when she took a ride in a hot-air balloon through the wine country of the Loire Valley and Burgundy. The balloon descended so everyone could do some wine testing and buy a bottle if they liked it. It sounded like something I could really get a kick out of. I really like flying. It all sounds to me like the French just have a love of life and leisure. After all, most only work 35 hours a week with five weeks of vacation.

The French philosophers believe in freedom, equality, and brotherhood. They are all one big happy family and all have basic rights that their rulers could never take away. France is a founding member of the United Nations, which protects human rights. France has a Statue of Liberty, which was given to the city in 1885. It faces west, towards the original Statue of Liberty in New York. It sounds like France represents a lot of what the United States started out like. After all, we did have a lot of French settlers in Louisiana.

It was still daylight when we pulled into the driveway and Cloie said, "The place looks great. I really missed it." Cloie went through every room in the house, as if each was welcoming her home, then grabbed a towel and headed out the back door. The scenery seemed to take her breath away. The flowers were in full bloom and the trees were green as poison. Coming up the path was Bam, my pet deer. Cloie dropped her towel on a lawn chair and went out to meet Bam. Cloie hugged Bam's neck and Bam seemed to wrap her neck around Cloie's shoulder. They truly were happy to see each other.

Cloie said to me, "Chelsea, Bam has really grown up. I wasn't sure she remembered me until she hugged me back."

I said, "That is a very intelligent deer." Cloie gave me a big smile and headed for the outdoor shower. I saw she forgot her towel and hung it on the door for her.

After everyone had their showers, Mom and Dad said their goodnights, but Cloie and I stayed up another two hours. I told Cloie that if Bam ever break's her leg and has to be put down that I would give her to a poor family so they could feed their children some very good deer meat. I could never eat Bam myself but there is no way I would let her be wasted on a bunch of low life worms. I let Cloie know that I shared her feeling about her horse Buddy. We both love our pets very much and we know that if they could talk, they would want to do some good for a family when their time on earth was up. With that shared moment we went to bed.

The next morning, Mom woke us up with breakfast in bed. She served us eggs and bacon with French Toast and orange juice. What a way to start the day. We should have plenty of energy.

As I walked out the back door I saw Bam in the oblique early morning sunlight and thought about how someday in the future, I would not be seeing Bam anymore. It was a very sad moment and I thought this must be how Cloie felt when she lost her horse Buddy. I grabbed a couple of jellybeans and held my hand out for Bam to see them. She came running and had a sweet bite that made her ears and tail wiggle. Whoever has Bam on the supper table will be having a mighty fine meal.

When I went back into the house Cloie said, "We should go looking for a car today for the birthday girl who will be turning 16 in just two days."

Dad said, "You two run along, I want to smoke some ribs for supper. Besides, you two have a lot of catching up to do."

We jumped in Cloie's jeep and off we went in the search for my wheels. I wouldn't consider anything but an American made car. I'm old fashion that way. I believe in taking care of your own whenever you possibly can. I may have to get a used car, but it will be an American made car. If I can find it, I specifically want a red Mustang.

Cloie pulled into a Ford dealership parking lot and we began to browse casually through the Mustangs. They were a fine group of cars ranging from brand new to ten years old. They had every color you could think of. I had my mind set on a red Mustang until I saw a beautiful turquoise Mustang with white interior. This car was a light, brilliant bluish-green that stopped me in my tracks. It was a color that only a Mustang could look this good in. I guess a girl has the right to change her mind on the color of car she wants. It was two years old and had my name all over it. We talked to the car dealer and agreed on a price. I gave him a down payment to hold it for me and said that I would be back in two days to pick it up. He gave me a certificate stating it was in tip-top shape. I was thrilled. It felt like a dream that in just two days I will be driving my own car, getting a job, and going on dates. Life is grand.

When we pulled into the driveway, the smell of smoked ribs filled the air. Cloie turned to me and said, "Now that's home cooking."

Mom said, "Did you girls have any luck finding a car?"

I excitedly said, "Yes, Mom, and in two days you will get to see my choice!"

Cloie said, "We hope she passes her driver's test. I must say that she has good taste in automobiles."

I said, "Ed was my teacher in Driver's Ed and he said I should pass with flying colors!"

Mom said, "Alright you two, let's get in the backyard. Your dad has a great meal waiting for you."

The ribs are simply delicious and the corn on the cob and fried okra were scrumptious.

Cloie said, "The French could take a lesson or two from my Mom and Dad on cooking. This food is heavenly." All this bragging on my parents cooking put a grin on both of their faces. Their smile was a self-conscious; a knowing they did well but still trying to be humble kind of smile. After all, cooking is a form of art that lasts only in the memory. You can't hang it on the wall. The praise must be immediate and the person preparing the meal should be told that their art is appreciated.

My parents are turning in early for they have to go to work in the morning. Vacation is over for them. Cloie and I did the dishes and went to bed early as well. We have a big day of fun planned for tomorrow. We said our goodnights and went to sleep.

Morning came early with the slam of the screen door. My parents were off to work. Two bagels with cream cheese and a pitcher of orange juice were left on the table for us for breakfast. After the big supper we had last night, this was all we needed. It really hit the spot.

"Grab your bathing suit and let's go swimming in Lake Tenkiller. After seeing that turquoise Mustang you picked out, my mind keeps thinking about the turquoise water of Lake Tenkiller when the sun hits it just right," Cloie said.

I said, "Great idea, we can jump off the cliffs on the

east side of the lake below the dam. On a hot day like today, the deeper we can dive, the colder the water, and I really enjoy the cold deep water."

We always swim in the early hours before the burning rays of the sun can damage our skin. The early morning sunrays are actually good for your body because they give you Vitamin D, which is essential for normal bone growth. Another means of getting Vitamin D is by eating fish. Our dad fishes in Lake Tenkiller often and provides the family with fish on a regular basis. The whole family believes in taking care of our bodies so we can have a long healthy life. After all, if you don't have good bones you won't have good health.

The water is cool on top and cold down deep today. I just dove off one of the cliffs and thrust my body forcibly into the deep dark depths of the lake. I went as far down as my ears could handle. When the pressure builds in my eardrums it tells me I've gone far enough. After going so deep in the coldest part of the lake, the surface water feels warm. Tenkiller is one of the deepest lakes in Oklahoma and therefore it doesn't get as warm as most lakes do in the height of summer.

As I swam back to the cliffs, Cloie was pointing towards the dam.

She said, "Look over there, I see some divers. Look, you can see the breathing apparatuses on their backs."

"Yes, I see them," I replied, "We need to try that someday! I hear the fish down there are longer than we are tall! Some say they look like monsters when they swim towards you!"

We took a few more dives off the cliffs and then lay on our towels to catch some rays. It was around 10 a.m. and the sun felt marvelous on our skin. As I looked up at the white fluffy clouds against the blue sky, one particular cloud stood out. I brought it to Cloie's attention.

As I pointed to the sky I said, "Cloie, I see the face of God looking down upon us. He seems to be smiling at our happiness. It's as if he is pleased that we are enjoying his creation."

Cloie said, "Yes, I see the face of God also. This is amazing! I feel so blessed to share this moment with you."

Just as quickly as it had formed the cloud began to drift apart and lose its shape. I will never forget what I saw today. God let me know he is pleased with me; I can feel it in my bones. This is a sign that will strengthen my faith in the Bible, which is God's Word. I believe that God approves of the way I live my life. I want to please God, and after today, my future plans are to improve, improve, improve. I need to help more people find God. That is what God put in my heart and head today. I believe he wants to use me as his tool to improve the world in which we all live.

The sun's rays are becoming stronger so we loaded up in the jeep and headed for home. When we got in the house the air conditioning in the house felt wonderful. It has been an extremely hot summer this year. Cloie said, "I think we should watch some TV until the air cools down some." I nodded my head and grabbed a seat. Halfway through the movie I must have fallen asleep because next thing I knew my mother was coming through the door.

"Did you girls have a good day?" she asked. Cloie immediately began to tell Mom how great the water was this morning at Lake Tenkiller. She hasn't seen Mom for a whole year and will only be home for a week so I give her plenty of catch up time. They moseyed leisurely off to the kitchen to fix a cup of green tea, which she always likes to have when she gets off work. She says it gives her natural energy.

An hour has passed and they are still in the kitchen catching up on stories when my dad walks through the door. He had the mail in his hand and tossed me an envelope with my name on it, Chelsea Songbird. I opened it and saw it was a birthday card from my good friend from school, BreAnna. She wished for me to have the best sixteenth birthday that anyone could have. It brought joy to my heart that she remembered.

Mom came out of the kitchen with Cloie right behind her and gave Dad a welcome home kiss. In the next breath she asked if he would like fish for dinner. He gave a nod and she handed him a cup of tea.

Mom rolls the fish in cornmeal and deep fries it in peanut oil. It smells so good. She has a large platter with catfish piled at least six inches high by the time she calls us to the kitchen to eat. The fresh tossed salad was passed in a clockwise direction followed by hushpuppies, a fried cornmeal fritter, corn on the cob, and fresh-cut cantaloupe. This is my favorite meal and Mom knows this about me. She must be doing this because tomorrow is my birthday and will be a very busy day. While we are having dinner I thought it would be a good time to tell my parents about the events of the day.

I started by telling my mother what a great dinner she had prepared for the family, and she gave me a smile and a nod of acknowledgement. I then moved on to tell her how Cloie and I went swimming in the very Lake these fish came out of. There was a chuckle from everyone at the table. I went on to say that while Cloie and I were sun bathing after two hours of swimming that I saw the face of God in a white fluffy cloud.

About this time, Cloie backed me up and said, "That's right, I saw it too. Chelsea brought it to my attention and I believe it was the face of God. He looked pleased."

My dad then said, "It looks to me like he has chosen you two to be his angels on earth. I hope you can live up to his expectations."

Chapter 2
Turning Sixteen

As I slowly woke up on this glorious morning, I remembered that I turned sixteen years old at approximately 2:16 a.m. Butterflies filled my stomach as I realized that in a couple of hours I would be taking my driver's test and if I passed, a Ford Mustang would soon be sitting in the driveway.

A soft knock at my door let me know someone else remembered this special day. I said they could come in, and as the door opened my mom, dad, and Cloie entered my room with a cake and sixteen candles burning. They began singing Happy Birthday with big smiles on their faces. I made a wish that I would pass my driver's test, and blew out the candles. They each gave me a hug and we cut the cake. It was my favorite kind: a banana nut cake. Cloie passed out the plates, Mom cut the cake, and Dad poured each of us a cup of coffee. Cake for breakfast doesn't sound like it is a very good start for the day, but the way my mom fixes it, the cake is healthy and nutritious. After all, bananas are healthy, and cream cheese icing is not too bad for you. I always have a banana nut cake for breakfast on my birthday.

Cloie said, "Sissy, get your clothes on. It's time to

take your driver's test!" She got no argument out of me. We loaded up in Cloie's jeep and hopefully we were headed for a blissful day. Mom and Dad stayed behind and promised to have lunch ready when we got home. Little did I know, their plan was to pay for my Mustang and have it in the driveway when Cloie and I returned. It didn't matter to them if I passed my driver's test or not; it was my birthday present either way. They knew sooner or later I would pass.

As Cloie pulled into the testing center for drivers, my heart rate picked up.

I said to Cloie, "My heart is in my throat and I'm having trouble breathing. I'm so scared that I won't pass!"

"Just relax like your teacher Ed taught you. Take a deep breath and push that heart out of your throat and back into your chest," said Cloie.

I took Cloie's advice and started getting control over my body. I signed up to take my test and we both took a seat. No sooner did we sit down then the person who would be testing me called my name. I stood up and started walking toward the man who called me.

"Chelsea Songbird?" he asked, "My name is Don and I will be observing your driving skills today."

I shook his hand and we headed for the jeep. I must have been the first person to be tested this early morning, which was fine by me. I think if I had to wait very long, a nervous disorder might have set in on me. Don was a nice man and made me feel at ease. I guess that is part of his job.

As I drove out of the parking lot Don gave me instructions to turn left and when we got to the traffic light to make a right hand turn. By him giving me instructions ahead of time it made things much easier. The mind is busy processing each step and this creates a feeling of being in control. Don let me pick the spot that I wanted to parallel park in. What a guy! He made this so comfortable for me that I made it on the first try. He told me I did outstanding.

By now I was flying high and confident that the scores on the test would be high.

Don asked, "Do you think you can find your way back to the office?"

I responded, "Yes, I believe I can."

This must mean that the test was over, and I was confident I had gotten a good score. The speed limit is 40 mph on the street back to the office and I was keeping an eye on my speedometer, when suddenly a squirrel darted out in front of the jeep and I ran over it. I felt like a thousand needles were sticking my entire body. I turned on my turn signal to pull over on the shoulder as the back tires made a thumping sound when the jeep ran over the squirrel for the second time. I slowed the jeep down and pulled over on the shoulder of the road and stopped the jeep. I hurriedly got out of the car, ran over to a grassy area and threw up.

I was shaking all over and Don handed me his handkerchief, and said, "Use this, it is clean." I wiped my mouth and handed it back to Don. He said, "That's alright, you can keep it. Are you alright?"

I said, "I'm okay. Let's get back to the office."

When we got back into the office, Don said, "Chelsea Songbird, if you will sit in the chair over there so that the young lady can take your picture for your driver's license, I will start the paperwork."

I said, "Thank you Don. I'm sorry for all of the drama."

"That's okay," he replied, "And by the way, you did exactly what you were suppose to do in that situation. You did not swing into head-on traffic to try to miss the squirrel. You ran over it and put the safety of people first."

Cloie heard the whole conversation and felt no need to make me relive the event all over again. With my driver's license in hand, we headed for home. As we pulled into the driveway, I saw the turquoise Mustang with a huge white ribbon tied from the hood to the bumper and from the driver's side door to the passenger side door. On top was a huge white bow. It was so beautiful it brought tears to my eyes. I ran and gave my parents a big hug and said thank you so many times I couldn't count them all. What an emotional day this has turned into!

Cloie went into the house and came out with a wrapped present and handed it to me. I opened the present and inside was a necklace that she handmade from white and turquoise beads. She told me it says, 'I love you' in the Cherokee language. She said she used her artistic ability to make it by hand for me.

I said, "I knew you made it the second I saw it. Its beauty is beyond words." I gave her a big hug and a kiss on the cheek. "Cloie, would you be so kind as to tie my necklace on in the back," I asked. She did and with that we went in for lunch.

Mom had a big pitcher of fresh squeezed lemonade on the table with sandwiches and cubed watermelon for dessert. After this nourishing lunch, I will unwrap my present from my parents and take everyone for a spin in my Mustang.

Dad said, "Miss Chelsea, how about you take the family to see the new Cherokee Nation casino in Tulsa? I know you are itching to drive that Mustang and we have been wanting to see the new casino."

I said, "What are we waiting for?"

Mom said, "Here are some scissors to cut the ribbon with. No need to waste it, we can use it for years to wrap presents. There's a lot of ribbon out there." I took the scissors from my mom's hand and hugged her neck. A snip here and a snip there and I was ready to put the keys in the ignition and start up the engine. This is so exciting to be able to be a chauffeur for my family.

Everyone loaded into my Mustang and Dad said, "Chelsea, you have very good taste in the color and style of cars. I really like this Mustang."

"Thanks, Dad. I am going to need some directions on how to get to Tulsa," I said.

Dad said, "No problem, just head north and follow the signs."

This car drives like a dream and I look so hot in it with my matching choker necklace. How wonderful it is that Cloie made me this necklace and it happens to match my car perfectly. As I thought about this I reached up and touched it.

I thought about the love that went into it and said to Cloie, "This necklace is so neat, I wanted to say thank you again for it. Everything about it is beautiful, from the design to the language to the work that you put into making it."

Cloie smiled and replied, "You're worth it, Chelsea."

I was driving with the greatest of ease and was very grateful that my family had complete trust in my ability to get them to Tulsa. The conversations were mainly about the fun times of our childhood, politics in the Cherokee Tribes, and how important the Cherokee language and symbols are to the Cherokees as a race. It is something passed down from preceding generations, and is part of our heritage; our status gained through birth. The Cherokee language is very dear to my father's heart, and today I vowed to learn to speak and write Cherokee so I can feel the deep connection my family feels. I am missing out on that part of life, but not for long.

We are now pulling into Tulsa and my GPS locator is showing how to get right to the new Casino.

As we pulled into the parking lot my dad said, "Look at the size of this thing! It's so tall!"

Cloie said, "Look, there's the restaurant McGill's! Do you two mind if me and Chelsea go there while you two try your luck and explore the Casino?"

Mom said, "You two run along and we'll see you in there in about an hour."

On our way up to the restaurant, Cloie and I saw

something we had never seen before. There was a huge swimming pool that was partially inside and partially outside. There was a glass wall separating the inside from the outside but the wall stopped once it reached the water, so people could swim underneath it to go back and forth. We stopped and watched people for a while in awe; this was something we were going to have to come back and try. Finally, the growling of our stomachs reminded us that we had been on our way up to the restaurant and we headed that way.

I had never been to McGill's but I had heard that it is especially good. I love a good hamburger and Cloie recommended the special that comes with fries and a drink. While waiting for our food, Cloie started telling me how grownup I look and act. She has been gone for over a year and I must really have changed during that time. Yes, I'm two inches taller and a year older, I wear make-up and always fix my hair. She's right, I realized, I do look different.

The waiter set our food on the table and it smells great. I love curly fries and these were fresh out of the hot oil. This burger is scrumptious, cooked to perfection, with a sesame seed bun. My taste buds are exploding.

I told Cloie, "Thanks for suggesting that we eat here, it is truly delicious."

"Things always hit the table hot at McGill's." Cloie said.

She had a point; fresh food is always good. After we finished eating we talked for about 30 minutes, and then decided to have some pie à la mode. This is where the pie is warm with a scoop of ice cream on top. I think the cherry pie à la mode sounds good. I'm a growing girl and can really eat. The ice cream is rich with strong vanilla flavor. The crust is light and flaky and the cherries are sweet with ripe cherry flavor. Everyone should have this meal at least once in their life.

Mom and Dad were walking up to our table about the

same time I was putting the last bite of cherry à la mode in my mouth.

Dad said, "How's the food?"

Cloie responded, "Not as good as what you cook, but it is still delicious."

Mom and Dad broke even in the casino, which is good for having an hour of entertainment. They grabbed a chair and ordered a burger to-go so we could get home before dark. I think they were trying to tell me something. They may have complete trust in me while driving during daylight hours, but they are unsure about nighttime driving.

While walking to the car, Dad noticed some dark clouds in the south. That just happened to be the direction we were going.

After everyone was in the car and seatbelts were on, Dad said, "Chelsea, do you know where your windshield wipers are and do you know how to get the windshield cleaner on the window?"

"No, Dad, I don't but before we take off I'm going to figure it out," I said.

Well it took me a while to figure it all out, but eventually I did. No need to wait until I get caught in a rainstorm. The clouds are getting darker and I turned on my lights to be sure others can see me. It is a safety measure that my parents noticed me taking and they gave me praise for doing so. My parents pay close attention to small details that their children take in life because they all add up. Caution in life adds up to being responsible and responsibility leads to having a favorable outcome.

The rain is coming down in sheets ahead. We haven't reached it yet, but it sure is dark ahead. The sky lit up every five minutes or so from the high-tension natural electric discharge in the atmosphere that we call lightning. When the lightning strikes you can see the rain clearly even though it is miles away. I'm so glad my parents have finished their to-go burgers; one of them may want to take the wheel out of my hand. I think this is something I can handle but they may be too nervous to let me try and handle it right after I got my license. I have never driven in the rain but there is a first time for everything.

Dad mentioned that turning on the radio instead of playing a CD might be a good idea. Someone in radio land might know what is going on with this rainstorm. After all, nothing was said about a storm on the weather channel this morning. I know because I checked the weather channel before taking my driver's test. I wanted every edge I could get on taking this test, and good weather was one of them.

I removed the CD, hit the radio button and then the seek button to find a local station. The broadcaster was saying, "There is a thunderstorm with a rotating column of air accompanied by a funnel-shaped downward extension of cumulonimbus clouds that has passed through Tahlequah and is now heading north. Extensive damage has been done by this rotating vortex that is several hundred yards in diameter whirling at destructive speeds of up to 200 miles per hour. This tornado contains baseball size hail that has left livestock in the Tahlequah area injured and some dead. So far no human fatalities have been reported. This tornado has taken a path through fields of soybean crops and cattle ranches. A farmer has reported a path that looks to be two blocks wide and five miles long that is nothing but brown dirt in the middle of his soybean crop. Another cattle rancher reported injury to his cattle from baseball size hail and the death of five new born calves. This storm can change direction at any time so stay tuned for live reports so you can take cover if it turns in your direction."

Dad said, "Our hometown is very lucky that the tornado didn't hit a populated area. What are a few beans and some veal from these calves in comparison to human lives? God has taken care of our people and our town. It looks like the storm is heading northeast and if it keeps going in that direction, we won't have to worry about driving into it. Chelsea, if you want to slow down a little I'm sure we will miss it unless it changes directions."

I said, "Sure, Dad. I'll slow down and if you want to drive it's okay with me."

"No, not right now. You're doing fine. If things get out of hand I'll consider it, but for now you are doing a great job," Dad said.

The bulk of the storm was east of us but we were starting to get some rain. I was glad my dad had me go through the steps of finding my windshield wipers before we headed into the storm. He has once again taught me how to be responsible and I love him for that.

As we drew near Tahlequah the hail was still on the street but had been reduced from softball size to the size of a quarter. The thought of being caught in the storm that produced all this hail with my birthday Mustang made my blood run cold. I was either very lucky or someone was looking out for me.

My thoughts were now on my doe, Bam, and her safety. I expressed this to my family and Dad said, "Bam has plenty of trees to get under for safety. Those poor cattle, on the other hand, are in an open field and will have no place to take cover."

Cloie said, "Speaking of Bam, in France they use citrus oil, lemon oil and lavender oil to make flea collars for their pets. They also give them B-vitamins so blood-sucking critters will stay off their pets. The French are much more health conscious than Americans. They burn candles made with basil, rosemary and bay leaves to keep flying insects away instead of spraying bug spray on their bodies when having cookouts. These things really work and they are natural."

Mom said, "I think I will make me one of those

candles for the next time I grill our supper outdoors. By the way, I love Bam, but I am more concerned about whether our house is still standing. That would be a tragedy if our home was destroyed."

As we got deeper into Tahlequah where the storm had started, I found myself having to dodge debris on the road. Tree limbs and power lines were on the roads for two blocks, then for five miles all would be clear, then there would be damage again for two blocks, then it would be all clear again. We had twenty more miles to go and it was like this all the way to our house. Hit and miss.

Dad said, "Do you think this tornado was jumping up in the air every five miles?"

We all said, "Yeah."

As I pulled into our driveway we saw our house was okay.

Mom said, "Thank you, God."

We all got out of the car and went to the backyard. The patio furniture had been turned over and scattered across the backyard. Some large limbs have been broken off of many of the trees. I do not see Bam anywhere, so I call her name. Over and over I call her name, but Bam was nowhere in sight. Maybe after things settle down, she will come out of the woods.

It was getting dark outside and we were all too tired to do any cleaning up of the fallen limbs. Mom and Dad have to go to work in the morning, so we had another piece of birthday cake and went to bed.

When I woke up in the morning Mom and Dad had already left for work and Cloie was still asleep. I went ahead and had the last piece of cake for breakfast. Bam was on my mind so out the door I went. I tried to get far enough away from Cloie's window so not to wake her. The backyard is a wreck with tree limbs everywhere. I moved enough limbs to clear a path to the wildlife refuge. I called for Bam for what seemed to be an hour but she never came to me. I decided to do something productive like pile up these limbs and put the patio table and chairs where they belong. A lot of progress had been made before Cloie woke up and joined me.

Cloie said, "Good morning Chelsea. The time change between here and France just caught up with me. I was just so tired." She had a cup of coffee in her hand and sat down at the patio table.

I joined her and said, "I can't find Bam."

Cloie said, "She is a deer and was made to survive outdoors. She is fine, I promise."

I continued to gather the broken limbs and pile them in a heap so we could navigate around the backyard. I just had to stay busy to keep my mind clear of thoughts that Bam could be hurt somewhere in the Wildlife Refuge. It is very large and if she could hear me calling her, she would come running, like always. I don't dare go in there and risk getting hurt or lost because everything is different since the storm came. The trails I take are covered with leaves and limbs from the trees. One of the beehives has been turned over and bees are flying all around it. The garden solar hot wire has a good size limb lying on top of it. That job I will have to leave for Dad to saw with the chainsaw. It's just too big for any of us to lift. It is truly amazing what a windstorm can do. It would take a lot of strength to bring down some of the limbs I've seen today. I hope Bam wasn't under any of them when they fell.

Cloie was calling my name, so she must want to spend some time with me. I need a break and by now she has fully woken up and should be ready for the day. I made myself a cup of tea and sat down on one of the chairs next to Cloie.

I said, "Cloie, if something bad has happened to Bam I don't think I will handle it very well. I am just really close to that deer."

"You know something Chelsea, humans always outlive their pets, unless it is one of those birds that live 200 years. You must enjoy them while you have them and when its their time to go, you must accept it. The fact is that no matter what, they only have at the most 15 to 20 years life expectancy. You could outlive as many as five pets in your lifetime," Cloie said.

Cloie has a valid point; I will definitely outlive Bam, but I want her to die of old age not from a tree limb falling on her. I think my next pet should be a bird. Perhaps an African Grey. I understand they can live longer than most people do. They can also talk and have a cute red tail. I can keep him in a cage and not have to worry about him.

Cloie changed the subject and asked me, "How was the trip to Florida?"

I responded with great enthusiasm, "It was wonderful. I swam in the ocean and surfed with a dolphin that swam circles around me. It was heaven on earth. Also I met this wonderful guy named Jeff. He is a mountain of a guy, at least 6 feet tall and very athletic. He's the one who taught me how to surf. He would take me by the hand and we would walk on the beach. Sister, when he held my hand it was the first time I have ever felt romance."

Cloie said, "This sounds serious."

I said, "He's much to far away for things to get serious, but when he held my hand, it was like I could feel his enthusiasm."

Cloie said, "Well, I've never heard it called enthusiasm, but that is a good description of a romantic feeling."

"You know Cloie, I have a lot of guy friends and I love them, but it's like friendship love. With Jeff it's different. From the moment I saw him it was just different. I could feel his enthusiasm even before he held my hand. When he took my hand it confirmed what I already felt in the air, only better. It was a giddy lighthearted silliness. I know he felt it also by the way he looked at me. It was an unspoken feeling. One interesting thing about him was that he had a group of friends who had all vowed to become centenarians, which are people who live to be 100 years old or older. They would have to live pretty clean lives to accomplish that. I really like these kinds of kids. I guess there is a lot to be said about birds of a feather flock together. You know Cloie, I think what I have is a crush on Jeff. It's the first time anyone has ever affected me this way," I said.

"Well little sister, welcome to the world of romance. It is truly a gift from God. However it can also be a double-edged sword. It can cause as much pain as it does pleasure. You will see what I mean when you are broken up with for the first time. In other words, the first time you are dumped. Most teens experience this at least once during their teen years. The reason for this is they are in a learning phase of their life. These wonderful feelings can be brought on because of the way someone looks or because of the sound of their voice. Teens fail to realize the importance of personality. If once you get to know them, and you find that you don't have anything in common, then the only alternative in the long run is to break up. You must understand that attraction at first sight can be very temporary. You see, teens are at the height of hormonal changes. Hormones create an urge. A hormone is a substance produced by one organ that is taken by the bloodstream to another, which is stimulated by chemical activity. A hormone is completely unaware of personality and is simply susceptible to infatuation. It is more like an animal instinct. God gave humans a mind, which should oversee our instincts and control our behavior. Teens generally learn this the hard way. A healthy relationship must depend on the ability to get along with the person you are spending time with. If you are attracted to someone but you do not like them, you are headed for a disaster. In my opinion, it takes at least six months to really know someone. Nevertheless, before you get too serious with a guy, you better know him or you risk getting a heartache. Believe me, the wait is worth it. The divorce rate is proof of what I'm saying. You may run across as many as seven guys that make you feel like Jeff does before you meet the one who is right for you. You must have common goals and share moral values. You know, like Mom and Dad do. They are a perfect example of what life has to offer. Family always comes first with them." Cloie said.

"You are jumping to conclusions. All I did was hold his hand!" I said.

"That's how it starts, with that little spark you said you felt when he took your hand. You two did not have that much time to spend together because it was just a two-week vacation. There is a lot of distance between the two of you right now, but you are talking like he is right here and you are holding his hand," Cloie said.

"Yes, you are right. It's as if he is right here. You would have to meet him to understand what makes him such a great guy. I don't plan on getting married to Jeff or anything like that," I said.

Cloie replied, "I know that sis, I just want you to know when you are 70 years old sometimes you will reminisce and have thoughts of Jeff. If indeed he is a great guy, you will have pleasant thoughts. If, on the other hand, he causes you harm you will remember the bad times. You see Chelsea, you always remember past experiences and I want nothing but good memories for you. This experience with Jeff is a new one and believe me, you will remember it forever. I'm glad he is far away because this will keep you from losing control."

"Come on, Cloie, I am a far cry from losing control. It's a great feeling and he is a good guy. I know when I am seventy years old that thoughts of Jeff will put a smile on my face. I may never see him again except in pictures, but I will always remember what a great vacation I shared with him this summer. If you ever get to meet him, Cloie, I know you would like him," I said.

Cloie hugged my neck and told me she loved me and she just wanted me to know that my safety is a big concern to her. I can't help but wonder if Cloie had her heart broken when she was my age. Why else would she be so aware of the pain involved in a break-up? I would not dare ask her on this little vacation of hers and bring back bad memories though. If she wants to talk about it she will have to bring it up.

With that little break I caught my second wind and started picking up limbs again. Cloie joined me and we made a lot of progress. We started clearing the path in the Wildlife Refuge that led to the pond. The whole time I was looking in the woods for Bam. Cloie noticed and gave a holler for Bam and then she looked back at me and smiled. Our goal was to clear a path all the way to the pond. We have a ways to go because we still cannot see it.

Our beautiful Wildlife Refuge is a disaster. Limbs are broken off the tops of the trees and are still hanging by just a string. It is a creepy feeling when you look up at them because we don't want to be working under a limb large enough to possibly kill us if it were to drop.

We worked for around two hours and it was time for another break. Cloie sat at the table and I made a pitcher of iced tea. It was starting to get warm outside so we need to keep plenty of fluids in our bodies. I poured us a tall glass of tea with a slice of lemon hanging half in and half out of the rim of the glass.

Cloie said, "Thanks sis, this is just what I needed. Looks like we have made some real progress, but we have a ways to go before we reach the pond. When we get there we might just take a dip. What do you think?"

"Sounds good to me. Maybe if we splash and make a lot of noise, Bam will come out and greet us. Until I know she is okay, she will constantly be on my mind," I said.

Cloie just smiled. She thinks Bam is just fine but I am concerned she could be hurt. We took a 30-minute break and then went back to work. Mom and Dad will be proud of all the progress we made. They didn't ask us to do all this; we just wanted to help clean up this mess.

Cloie said, "Sis, I see the pond! We don't have much further to go; maybe just another hour. That storm must have been right on top of this Wildlife Refuge. I have never seen so many broken limbs."

Cloie is so selfless. Here she is on her vacation helping me clear a path to the pond because I think Bam will come and get a drink and I will then know for sure she is okay. I am so lucky to have a family that cares about each other's worries.

We finally made it to the pond and cleared out the debris around the bench and sat down. We both had sweat on our foreheads and were tired from all the hard work. To my amazement, the pond had very little debris in it. It was almost like it was untouched. A welcoming sight if I may say so myself. I looked around for Bam and called her name, but had no luck just yet in finding her. We decided to take a dip in this beautiful spring-fed pond as a reward for all the hard work we had endured for the day, and it felt great.

Chapter 3
Summer is Ending

When Mom and Dad came home from work they were so impressed with the cleanup job Cloie and I had done on the backyard. We had two piles of limbs that were higher than we were tall.

Mom said, "Is that a trail we see in the woods that lead to the pond?"

I quickly answered, "It is! We cleared a path to the pond and then took a swim. I thought Bam would have an easier time getting home this way. We have yet to see hide or hair of her."

Mom said, "Don't worry, animals have a way of taking care of themselves. I'm sure she is fine." I hope my mom is right. Thoughts of what Cloie had to do with her horse kept jumping into my mind. They just came out of nowhere and I really tried to suppress the thoughts and keep them from my conscious awareness. It is as if I have no control over my thoughts.

Dad said, "Girls, come jump in the truck. I want to show you what that storm did on the outskirts of town."

This is just the distraction I needed. Going for a drive. Dad had heard on the radio where the twister had destroyed a barn that belonged to a friend of his, and he wanted to offer his friend some help. The closer we got to his friend's place the worse the damage to trees and structures were. We saw a tractor wrapped around a tree. What we were seeing did not even make sense. It looked impossible but yet it was a fact. The tractor was actually wrapped around the tree.

When we got to the house of my dad's friend, the house looked intact but his barn was completely gone. Not even one piece of the barn was left. Nothing that was in the barn was anywhere to be seen. The dirt floor was the only thing left. I'm truly amazed that no one died due to the force of this twister. My dad let his friend know that he would help in any way he could, and to just let him know a couple of days in advance. And with that we headed back home.

My family is very lucky the damage is only to the trees. Some of the people have lost their homes and cars. Hopefully they all have insurance. For those who don't, like my father's friend, he will call on his Native American friend for help. The Native American culture is always willing to help each other. One for all and all for one is our motto. We help where help is needed.

On our way home we talked about the force of nature. This is one thing mankind will never be able to control. We will just have to respect it and protect ourselves with the proper shelter.

Cloie will be going back to France soon to finish her studies in language. I want to make the most of her last two days with her family. I told Cloie, Mom, and Dad to go sit in the backyard while I fix dinner. They needed to spend some relaxing time together. I watched out the kitchen window as I poured water into a pot to boil spaghetti. They were laughing and having a great time. A bottle of white wine and three glasses were on the way.

Dad said, "Chelsea, that's just the best idea, thank you."

He put the corkscrew in, popped the cork, passed it around for everyone to smell, and then poured the wine. I smelled the cork and that is the closest I came to any wine. Back in the house for me. The water is now boiling and it's time to warm the chicken. I used canned white meat; this makes for an easy meal. The sauce covers the taste of everything so it must be the best money can buy. I like the garden combination because that way we get a balanced meal. I put garlic bread in the oven and the meal is complete. With two plates in my hand, out the door I went.

"Guests and ladies first," I said.

Dad smiles at me approvingly. Soon I was back out the door with his and my plate.

Cloie said, "Little sister, you have become quite the chef while I was away. This is delicious!"

I replied, "Thank you for noticing. This is a very healthy meal with wheat spaghetti, lean white chicken breast and vegetable sauce."

Mom said, "I taught you well."

If I may say so myself, this really is a good plate of spaghetti and the garlic bread is my favorite part of the meal. It felt so good to cook for my family and then do the dishes so they could spend some quality time together. After I finished cleaning the kitchen I reached up and touched the necklace on my neck that Cloie made me for my birthday. She put a lot of love and thought into this present and I said to myself, "I love you too."

It's time for me to join my family and have some fun.

Cloie said, "Sis, come sit by me, I was just telling Mom and Dad what a great time I was having being home with the family. It's going to be difficult to leave."

Dad said, "It's harder on this side. As a matter of fact it's three times harder because there's three of us. You need to come home again for Christmas."

Cloie answered smiling, "We'll see."

Mom and Dad said their goodnights and me and Cloie stayed up to talk about all that had happened over the past year while we were apart. Cloie seemed to be interested in my feelings for Jeff. Yes, it was the first time any boy has gotten my attention in that way. He keeps creeping into my thoughts. He must be thinking about me and I can feel it. I think I should check my email to see if he has left me any messages. Cloie encouraged me to check it and asked if I had a picture of him. I told her he gave me his address and his MySpace and I bet I could show her a picture of him on there.

Cloie said, "Let's check his MySpace before anything so that I can see what he looks like." Cloie is pretty smart. She wants to know my taste in guys and figured she should see a picture of him to help her figure that out.

When his picture came up the first thing she said is, "He looks like he could be Native American. Is he?"

I said, "I think you could be right, but I didn't ask him. That could be part of the reason I am so attracted to him."

Cloie said, "I think he is definitely Native American. He is very handsome. Sis, you have good taste as far as looks go. I also like how he wears his football uniform with his helmet tucked under his arm so we can see his face."

I said, "This is so strange, he didn't tell me his whole family was on his MySpace. He told me one of his brothers played college football for Texas, but Texas has several football teams. His oldest brother has a drug problem and Jeff is very disappointed in him. You can tell he has a problem in this picture. His dad definitely is Native American."

Cloie said, "You see that Bull with those long horns? His name is Bevo and he is the mascot for Texas University. When Oklahoma plays Texas it is called bedlam. A bedlam game is a place of noisy uproar and chaotic confusion. Someday I will take you to one of their games so you can see what I am talking about. You have to be at the game to appreciate the bedlam in the air."

I said, "Cloie, I would love to go to a bedlam game with you. I could introduce you to Jeff's brother and maybe we could do a double date."

Cloie said, "That sounds like fun. They both look big and strong."

I said, "I told you that when Jeff held my hand I could feel his strength seeping into me. It was an amazing feeling that keeps me thinking about it all the time."

Cloie said, "I'm glad he is in Texas. That will keep you safe from yourself. Not much can happen over the computer."

I said, "You should really have more faith in your little sister. I have a lot of control over my actions. My mind is another matter, but I am working on it. My thoughts are pure but very exciting."

I'm having a great time talking about Jeff with my big sister. This is the first time I've talked like this to her and I'm having a blast. Times like this make me want her to go to school in Oklahoma, but I know she wants the experience of being on another continent. I would never ask her to alter her education plans for me. That would be selfish.

When I check my email Jeff had left me two messages. The first asked if I made it home okay and the second was wishing me a Happy Birthday.

"Isn't that the sweetest thing you ever heard?" I said.

"When you feel the touch of a hand the way Jeff touches you, everything he does from now on will be the sweetest thing ever," Cloie said.

Cloie knows about these things because she has been dating for years and has experience with feelings that are new to me; therefore I will listen closely to what she has to say. I showed Cloie the seashell with the hole in it that Jeff found on the beach and gave to me. Cloie told me to always keep it safe because every time I see it, I will remember the feelings Jeff aroused by just holding my hand. She is so right because when I am a centenarian, 100 years old, I will get this seashell out and say, "Thank you, Jeff, for giving me the goal of becoming a centenarian." Before meeting Jeff I didn't even know what a centenarian was. Jeff challenged me to set it as one of my goals in life and if I make it to my 100th birthday, Jeff will get full credit.

I think a picture of me standing next to my Mustang with the beaded necklace Cloie gave me would be appropriate to send Jeff since he did mention my birthday in his email. I will let him know I am not bragging, but that I am just excited about life and want to share it with him. In this email he has to know what a great time we shared and that I miss the touch of his hand on mine. I need to know if he felt what I felt. If the feelings I am having are only on my side, I need to know.

The email read like this: "So good to hear from you and glad you remembered my birthday. Sending you a picture of my birthday presents. Mom and Dad got me the Mustang and my sister Cloie made me the necklace. My necklace says I love you in Cherokee. Cloie handmade it with love in her heart, so it is very special to me. I had a great birthday. By the way, you made my vacation a blast. Thank you for all of the fun we had. I miss the touch of your hand on mine. You gave me all the confidence and assurance in the world to surf with the best of them. Hope to hear from you soon."

It was just moments after I had clicked to send the email when I got a reply from Jeff. He must have been online or something.

He replied, "Nice car! You will look hot riding around on those nice wheels. That necklace must have taken forever to make. You are one lucky girl. I miss the touch of your hand also, but for a different reason. I felt a vibe that is new to me and I liked it. Football practice has started and it sure is hot. On vacation when we got this hot we could always take a dip in the ocean or pool, but out here on the field the shower is the only place to go to cool down. I miss the ocean, and I miss you."

I was so excited to read that Jeff felt the same way I did. I had to share it with Cloie immediately. She was excited for me but told me to keep a close watch on my heart. I told her she could be my mentor, a wise and trusted counselor for me. She was beaming with pride that I would share such a personal experience with her and that I would ask her to play such an important role.

Cloie said to me, "Sis, if you ever need to talk to me, just call or email me and I will be there for you. Enjoy the ride of your life because you will be sad when you are missing him and on the top of the world when you are talking to him."

I am so lucky to have someone I trust to give me advice. Someone who has been where I am going and who can help me deal with my feelings. I am so excited that Jeff felt the same as me. He was brave enough to tell me what he was feeling and that is fantastic. I am not sure if telling Jeff I feel the same vibe that he does is the right thing to do though so soon in the relationship.

Cloie told me that I should always be honest about my feelings. She told me I don't need to tell Jeff unless he asked me about them, if I am uncomfortable. A little mystery can even make things exciting.

I emailed Jeff back and told him about my sister coming home for my birthday and how she would be going back to France in a couple of days. I sent a picture of Cloie and Jeff suggested that she might make a good catch for his brother, who was also a football player. He said we should double date sometime, which was funny since I had said the same thing.

I showed this email to Cloie and she said, "When I

get back home that will be a date." We caught Jeff off guard by agreeing to the double date immediately; he had no idea I was sharing all of this with Cloie. I let Jeff know that the next couple of days I would be hanging out with Cloie constantly and might not have time to email.

It's getting late and Cloie suggested we say our goodnights. I gave her a hug and went to my room. I thought about what a great time I am having with Cloie and how it would be fun to double date with Jeff and his brother. Jeff is right; we should definitely double date. They would make a great couple. I think this is worth putting some effort into. If Cloie comes home for the holidays, this could happen. With that sweet thought I closed my eyes and went to sleep.

Cloie was knocking on my bedroom door to wake me up.

She was saying, "Chelsea, Chelsea, someone is here to see you!"

I said, "Tell them I am getting dressed," as I drowsily got out of bed. I opened my bedroom door and Cloie was waving me to the back door. I rubbed my eyes and as I got closer to the sliding glass doors I saw the form of Bam in all her glory. She was waiting for her jellybean. I couldn't help but yell her name with joy. I felt myself moving briskly out the door to hug her neck. She was just as excited to see me as I was to see her. Bam kept nudging my hand for a treat, and Cloie noticed so she grabbed a handful of jellybeans and put them in my hand. Bam smelled them and forced my hand open. As she chewed on jellybeans her tail began to wiggle. I looked over her to see if she had been hurt anywhere, but she looked just fine. Not a mark on her.

Cloie said, "She must have been so scared with all of the trees falling and the big storm with the twister putting all of that pressure in the air. Somehow I just knew she would come home though."

Seeing Bam again put instant joy in my heart. The

fear for her safety was lifted. I can enjoy my last full day with Cloie without anything clouding my happiness.

"Hey, Cloie, do you want to go get a bite to eat? I'll drive." I said.

Cloie grabbed her purse and guided me toward the door. I dipped down and grabbed my purse off the table next to the door and off we went, out the door and into my Mustang. It was closer to lunch than breakfast so I think a steak sandwich with fries would be perfect. It feels good to be driving my big sister around. She is at my mercy! I don't think she minds because I have good taste in food and fun.

After lunch a game of putt-putt would be fun. This is like golf only with small 10-foot greens. After eating that huge steak sandwich, this is perfect. It is slow moving so we can digest our food, plus we can have some good conversation. Since Cloie is sharing advice and guiding me in my first romance, I think it is appropriate for me to find out about her first romance.

So I asked her, "Cloie, tell me about the first guy that you really liked."

Cloie answered, "Well, sis, he was a football player and I was 16. We were crazy about each other. He was the first guy I ever dated, but he had been in love with a different girl the year before I met him. She had moved to another state though and just dropped out of his life. He became a one-woman man for a year after his love left town and I was that woman. Then his first love moved back home and he dropped me like a hot potato. When I first saw them walking down the hall hand in hand, my heart broke in half and it felt like the blood was running out of my body. My friends told me I turned white as a ghost. There were times after that when I thought I would faint when I saw them together. It was devastating, to say the least.

Something had to give though so I threw a party to help me get over their reuniting. I only invited 20 teens, but

I swear there must have been 50 people that showed up. The party was a blast. Dad had to move the furniture to one corner of the living room so that we could all dance. Two hours into the party, the heartbreaker himself walked in through the front door, girlfriend in hand. They thought I would greet them, but I chose to ignore them. Everyone at the party was fully aware of why I had thrown the party in the first place, so the guys made sure I had someone to dance with the entire time those two were there. It was so great to have so much support. This is why I have offered you my support if you ever need it with Jeff.

Anyway, I got past the whole thing eventually. A year later, they broke up and he came back to me wanting to be together again. No such luck for him because he had ruined all of the feelings I had for him with what he did to me. This is why you should always be tender with your heart when someone says they care about you. If you want to break up with someone you should tell that person kindly and give him time to get over you. No one should find out they are being broken up with by seeing him with another girl. That is just wrong. I lost all respect for him when he did that and I could never be with someone I didn't respect.

Now you know why I am so concerned about your first crush. I don't want you to get hurt the way that I did. It took me a whole year to get past it, and the pain and humiliation that came from it really hurt my heart and my pride. I derived great pleasure from turning him down for a date when he asked me after he had been dumped."

I had no idea my sister had gone through such a bad experience. I feel so sorry for her. If I had any idea about this I wouldn't have asked her about it so that she wouldn't have to relive it. I think it is time to change the subject. I was just a kid but I remembered the party she was talking about. Everyone had seemed like they were having such a good time. Now I know everything is not always what it seems to be.

I said to Cloie, "Thanks for sharing that with me. That seems like a very valuable life lesson that I will always keep close to my heart. I am sorry you had to experience such grief in you life."

Cloie said, "It's okay sis, it is truly in the past now, but at the time it was very hurtful."

The putt-putt game was a lot of fun and now that it is finished we have just enough time to take a five-mile float down the Illinois River in a canoe. It is one of our favorite things to do during the summer. The river is high because of the rains this week. That makes for great rapids that will carry us down the river with only a minimal amount of rowing on our part. The water is cold and very refreshing when the rapids splash us from the fast-moving steep descent in the riverbed full of bubbles. Many inexperienced people have turned their canoes over in the rapids after the rains.

The river has made a very large indention in the earth's crust, which makes the banks in some places as much as 30 feet high. This makes for a great wind block. Summertime on the river has the trees and shrubs as green as poison. When the canoes got past the rapids, the river became deeper and darker green with an occasional swirl to let us know we were still moving. The tranquil feeling that this river can give frees the mind of any agitation that life can sometimes create. It has a way of making you one with nature as you listen to the birds singing and an occasional bullfrog jumping into the water and making a splash that gets your attention. No words are necessary to describe what one is feeling because floating down the river leaves you speechless. Words would only detract from the peaceful surroundings. This river is truly one of God's gifts to mankind.

As we passed under the iron bridge we knew our five-mile trip was coming to an end. We looked at each other and just smiled to say, that was wonderful. The sun was rapidly dropping as we pulled into the driveway of our home.

Cloie sighed happily and said, "Chelsea Songbird, I want to thank you for a magical day. It was nice to be with my little sister rowing down the Illinois River with the tapestry of oak trees high on the hills. That was truly a spectacular sight to see. Thank you for a great day."

I was beaming, knowing that my sister had such a good time with me. I reached my hand to my necklace that she had made me for my birthday and then gave Cloie a big smile. She grabbed me and hugged me close. It brought happiness to my heart. Family is so important in my life and I truly cherish my time with them. They feed my soul.

Mom and Dad were patiently waiting for our return on the front porch swing. It is Cloie's last evening with the family because this time tomorrow she will be on a plane to France.

Mom hollered out, "Did the two of you have a good day?"

Cloie replied, "The best."

This filled my heart with joy to hear my sister say that. We all went into the house to have dinner. Mom set the table with her best china and silverware. This means that we are having a special meal, for Mom only brings these out when we are celebrating special occasions. We took our seats and Mom pulled out a roast from the oven covered with potatoes and carrots, one of Cloie's favorite dishes. "Mom, thank you so much. This makes a perfect end to my last night with my family until the holidays." Cloie said.

"So does that mean you are coming home for Christmas?" Mom asked slyly. "Well, I have a part time job in a gift shop that could pay for my transportation home and I get two weeks out of school for the holidays, so I just might be able to." Cloie said smiling.

Dinner was fabulous; a real treat to the taste buds. What was even better was that Cloie would most likely be home for the holidays. It just wouldn't be the same without her. Christmas has a way of making a very cold month seem warm and cozy. The back patio gets decorated to the hilt and has an old world charm to it. Sometimes at night we bundle up and sip hot tea while sitting on the patio furniture. The house and trees block the cold wind, which makes sitting outside tolerable. Without the trees blocking the wind we would not be able to endure the adverse environmental conditions that December brings. I don't think the twister will have an effect on our late night Christmas tea party even though it took out a lot of trees.

After I finished the dishes and Mom and Dad had spent some time with Cloie, I went into the computer room to check my emails. Jeff had sent me three messages. The first one asked if I had a webcam so we could see each other while we talked. His brother, the football player from the University of Texas just installed one on their computer. I replied that yes, we did have one, and that I was glad to see that he had finally come out of the dark ages and gotten one as well since we have had this technology for over a year.

The second email said he was eager to see me and if I didn't have a webcam I should go purchase one immediately. My reply was that it was truly amazing how fast technology was evolving and improving. The third email was saying how much Jeff missed me and how he wished he could hold my hand again. He talked about the amazing energy he felt between us, and told me he had dreamt about me. He said that it felt so real he had to pinch himself to bring him back to reality.

About the time I finished reading Jeff's emails, he had sent me another one. I felt a rush of excitement, because he wanted to video chat and was obviously online at that moment. I am so thrilled but at the same time a little frightened by his honesty. I have the very same feelings he has. The way I feel is so new to me that I am not sure how to respond to it. First, I must brush my hair and put on some lip-gloss. I want to look good. After I got ready, I clicked the mouse and we were talking live via video chat.

The first thing Jeff said was, "You look amazing! I wish I could be there with you right now."

My response was, "It is good to see you too. I had a very full day with Cloie today. It is her last full day with us. We went out to eat, played some putt-putt, and took a five-mile trip down the Illinois River in a canoe. My mom fixed roast for dinner and I did the dishes. I thought my parents needed some alone time with Cloie so I was just checking my messages. I just finished reading your last message, and I was going to say that I miss you too."

There was a gentle knock on the door and Cloie entered the room. I turned to her and pointed at the computer to indicate that I was video chatting. Cloie waved at Jeff and he waved back.

Then he said, "Hey Cloie. There is someone here who wants to meet you. This is my brother, Matt. Matt, this is Chelsea's sister, Cloie." They waved at each other and seemed to be studying each other's faces. There is something in the air between them already; I can feel it. They are in awe of each other. I see various emotions in my sister's face; I believe the word satisfaction would describe it.

Cloie said, "If you are anything like your brother Jeff you are alright in my book, Matt."

He laughed and replied, "Jeff got his values from yours truly. We made a pact 10 years ago to make a positive impact on this earth even if it is only microscopic. If every human being tried to leave a positive impact on our planet and on the people who occupy it, mother earth will be a happier and more carefree place for future generations. Does that make me alright in your books?"

"Yea, I think you are an okay guy," Cloie said, "Are you Native American?" Matt replied, "Actually, my father is full Cherokee. My brother tells me you live in Tahlequah,

Oklahoma, which is home to the Cherokee nation. I can tell that you are Cherokee as well."

Cloie replied, "You are right, both of my parents are Cherokee. This must be part of why Jeff and Chelsea are so attracted to each other."

"You know, Cloie, you are someone who I would like to get to know better," Matt said.

Suddenly Jeff jumped back into the picture and asked Cloie and Matt to say their goodbyes. They waved at each other and departed, so now it's just Jeff and I. This is so exciting! I made a brave move and again suggested to Jeff that maybe someday we could double date. I let him know that Cloie signaled me with a wow, meaning she thought Matt was handsome, and I let Jeff know that I thought he was handsome himself. This was a major move on my part. I think because he is so far away, and we are on computers, that I am braver than I normally am. There is energy in the air from all the attraction between the four of us.

Jeff said, "You know Chelsea, I would very much like to kiss you. If you had been sixteen when we were in Florida, I would have. I made a vow to never kiss a girl younger then sixteen to my parents. It is very important to them to protect the young, not that sixteen is old or anything, but girls are more mature at sixteen and most are allowed to date by then. I really had a difficult time controlling myself around you."

I said, "You know, Jeff, when you hold my hand I can feel your energy. That has never happened to me before. I think we should date because we are just right for each other. Obviously there is an attraction between Cloie and Matt. They were rather transparent with their emotions. I really think they would make a lovely couple."

To my amazement, the words are just flowing out of my mouth. It is like an out of body experience. Life is great. We talked for another 30 minutes and then said our goodnights. I wanted to spend more time with Cloie and talk about Jeff and Matt to her before we had to go to sleep. The morning will come early because Cloie has to catch an airplane in the afternoon heading to France. I will miss her.

When I closed the door to the computer room Cloie was right in front of me with a huge smile on her face.

She said, "Can there be such a thing as an incorruptible human beings? Because these two guys seem to be flawless."

I said, "They have a big brother who is a drug addict and they hate that. Jeff said to me this summer, 'Why would any teen feel the need to scruff up his squeaky-clean image with drugs? Why drop down to that level? There is no reasoning with drugs. They own you. The betrayal of reason is a crime against oneself. Drugs are a crime against oneself.' Jeff says you must police yourself because your memories will haunt you or will make your heart rejoice. It is your choice; you make your own history. Jeff cherishes his freedom from his brother's self-serving ways that are drug induced. Jeff and Matt cannot choose who their family is but they can choose how they conduct themselves.

They both have a really tough time with their big brother being a drug addict. They are always praying for Ed to get off the drugs. They believe that the sick people, and they do consider him to be sick, who are prayed for recover faster then those not prayed for. This is because we are all connected by the same field of consciousness. Jeff says that in studies of identical twins, they sense what is happening to each other at a distance. If twins can do this, he believes that brothers also can do this if they try hard enough. They hope to be able to reach Ed and bring him back to where he was before the drugs took control of his being. Drugs are evil, and evil dwells where there is a lack of love, which is why they continue to pray for their brother and show him love. We all have God inside of us, including Ed, we just need to get in touch with ourselves and experience the extraordinary clarity God has given us. Ed feels guilty that he cannot quit doing drugs and Satan wants him to feel guilty. It is Satan's ultimate goal.

Jeff quoted Matthew 7:13-14, which says, "Enter through the narrow gate. The gate that leads to damnation is wide, the road is clear, and many choose to travel it. But how narrow is the gate that leads to life, how rough the road, and how few there are who find it!" Jeff wants to help Ed find the narrow road that leads to life. He puts his words in a box and gift-wraps it for Ed, for it is a gift of knowledge that will help Ed get off the drugs.

Jeff also quotes John 8:34; "I tell you the truth, everyone who sins is a slave to sin." Drugs are a sin against oneself. Jeff said that he would never give up on Ed. He forgives him for being a drug addict because forgiveness leads to happiness and you have to forgive your entire life.

You know Cloie, if you were a drug addict I just don't know if I could find happiness. Jeff and Matt must be really strong guys to handle this situation," I said.

"We must learn to love all of life and not just one part of it. They love their brother even with all his faults. The power of love will allow you to accept faults in others. The way Jeff and Matt want to help their brother Ed is essential to the healing that only love can attain. Ed is brainsick and if they can reach him they can bring him back to reality. Drugs are a psychological torture and a weapon used against the mind. They beg you to take them when you are an addict. They have limitless powers that hold on to the addicted person who cannot find the larger meaning of life. They deteriorate the ability to control one's life with daunting speed. This is why you have to want to quit and you must seek help, to stay off of drugs.

I've never understood why anyone would risk becoming and addict. Like you said, they become a slave to the drug and the United States of America has fought worldwide to end slavery and promote freedom. Why would anyone subject themselves to becoming a slave to drugs. I just don't understand that mindset," Cloie said.

"You know Cloie, Jeff and Matt have learned a valuable lesson firsthand by seeing their brother Ed fall under the influence of drugs, and they have gained a greater appreciation for the road to right-mindedness. Their views and ideas are based on what is right and honest, and it runs in their views. They are making up for what their brother Ed has lost in life. That passion for what is right and what is good in life is what attracted me to Jeff, and now I see his brother Matt helped mold him, kind of like the way you molded me. It must be fate that has brought us together with Jeff and Matt," I said.

Whatever brought all of us together, I am thankful for it. It is an amazing feeling I get when I hear from or see Jeff. I get all giddy and get a lighthearted flighty feeling. No one has ever had that effect on me. I now know what my best friend BreAnna is talking about when she is with Jake. It is like having a whole different personality taking over your body. I have to get to know myself all over again. When Jeff talked about wanting to kiss me in Florida, I wonder why it never entered my mind. Maybe it was because just holding his hand was so intense that it was all I needed. I have never been kissed on the mouth, and I cannot even imagine what it would be like. My parents and sister kiss me on the cheek and forehead but that is completely different from how a kiss from Jeff would be. If his kiss will make me feel even better than it does when he holds my hand, then let the fireworks begin.

"Chelsea, if I were you, I would make sure Jeff doesn't have a girlfriend in Texas. He and his brother are awfully handsome to not have girlfriends. Let me know if Matt is involved with a girl. He sure is bold with his talk. If we are to double date when I come home for the holidays, I want to be sure there isn't someone getting their heart broken because of me." Cloie said.

I never even thought about Jeff possibly having a girlfriend in Texas. Cloie has my mind going all over the place right now. Is Jeff holding some other girl's hand, and she is getting that amazing feeling? Or even worse, is she sixteen and he is kissing her? I am feeling jealous simply over these images in my head. This is crazy. What is wrong with me? I am being suspicious and questionable of Jeff's intentions toward me and we are not even dating yet. I must clear my head and ask him if he already has a girlfriend, and then go from there.

I was the first to wake in the morning, so breakfast was on me. First the coffee pot was put on and then the bacon hit the pan. The smells filled the air and next thing I knew, Mom and Dad stumbled in and filled their mugs with coffee. Mom said she would wake Cloie and poured another cup of coffee before she went. Dad sat at the table and was rubbing his head and eyes.

He said to me, "How's my little Songbird this morning?"

My reply was, "I am just chirping along with bacon and eggs. Mom needs a break, so I decided to get things rolling for the day. I have the best breakfast planned for us. Bacon and eggs and waffles topped with butter and honey."

Dad said, "It sounds and smells delicious. Did you and your sister have a good time yesterday?"

I said, "We had a blast! Last night when I checked my email, Jeff had sent me some mail and he said he got a webcam so we video chatted! He introduced Cloie to his brother Matt. Just like the satellite station that immediately rebroadcasts a received transmission on a different wavelength, Matt and Cloie were rebroadcasting their likes for each other. You would think they wanted to be eternal lovers. They definitely are on the same wavelengths."

Dad looked at me and rolled his eyes. That was more information than he wanted to know this early in the morning.

Mom and Cloie poured another cup of coffee and sat at the table. I filled their plates with breakfast as they joined Dad and I. Cloie started off the conversation with questions about next year's vacation. Cloie would be out of school and joining us for vacation.

Mother is the one who is in charge of financing vacations and she started off the conversation with, "You know, its my turn to pick the vacation spot this year, and I have decided to keep it closer to home. We have always financed the bulk of our vacation with the honey from our beehives, we just don't have many bees anymore. We will be lucky to get enough honey for our personal use, let alone sell $1,500 worth of honey to the stores. The storm has also turned over the beehives and disrupted them as well. I was checking out the problem on the Internet and there is a shortage of bees all over the United States. I have figured that we save $704 a year by drinking tea instead of soft drinks, which is $2 a day. We also save $1,760 a year by not smoking cigarettes, counting 1 pack a day. This is how I have always justified our expensive vacations. If the bees don't come back this year we will probably take diving lessons at the YMCA and go diving at Lake Tenkiller next summer. How does that sound?"

Cloie said, "That sounds exciting! I have always wondered what it looks like under the water near the dam. People come from all over to dive in these clear waters. Its about time we check it out."

I washed the dishes while Cloie packed her bags. Mom and Dad stepped out onto the backyard patio and finished drinking the last of the coffee. Bam was right there to meet them and both were talking to Bam and were so happy to see her. The days she was missing concerned all of us. Life is so fragile you never know what can happen, especially when Mother Nature is in control.

I took charge and started up my Mustang and popped the trunk open. Cloie loaded her bags in the trunk and we were off to Tulsa where Cloie would take a plane to Dallas and then change planes for her international flight to France. This was the best birthday week of my life. A new car, my sister coming home, and getting to video chat with Jeff. All of this was so exciting that I am riding high on life.

We arrived at our destination and Cloie was giving us hugs goodbye. We would be seeing her again in four months but it was still hard to see her leave. We had a group hug and with that Cloie was off to France.

The ride home was solemn but much better than a few days earlier when the storm was at hand. Dad asked if I would mind dropping by his friend's house who had completely lost his barn. I was more than happy to check on dad's friend. When we pulled up he was trying to put the barn back together, so we all chipped in with some help. Mom and myself held the tin in place while dad and his friend nailed it. By the time we finished we had all four walls up and all that was left was the door and roof. Dad told his friend he would be back in the morning to help him put on the roof.

It felt good physically to use our bodies and good mentally to help someone in need. Helping each other in need is the Cherokee way. It's just the natural thing to do.

The sun was beginning to set and a plane flew across the setting sun and thoughts of Cloie crossed my mind. She had a long way to go; almost to the other side of the world. When it's daytime here in America, it's dark in France. That is just amazing to me. I hope she has a good flight.

When we got home, I checked my email and Jeff had left a short message. He told me goodnight and let me know how good it was to see me and get to talk to me yesterday. I blew a kiss at his message and turned in for the night.

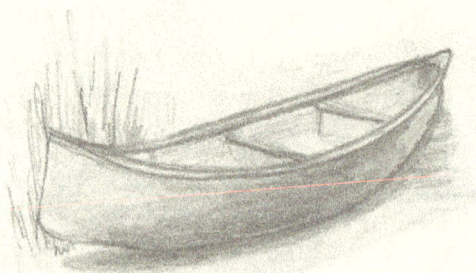

Chapter 4
Enrollment

BreAnna called me early in the morning to let me know our high school was offering a philosophy class that would be perfect for all our friends. Philosophy is the analysis and critique of fundamental beliefs as they come to be conceptualized and formulated. In other words, the overall values by which one lives. She is so right. We would have a blast sharing our beliefs and letting our imaginations roam. The secret to our friendship is our ability to combine each other's individual creativity into one large vision. We could share this with others in the philosophy class.

Consistency of metaphors is a good way to get your point across, and we all have that ability. We study history to learn from other's mistakes or successes, which helps us understand that a person's character will determine their destiny.

In a philosophy class we could challenge the class with a question, "Why not join the intellectual world that dramatizes what teens are lacking?"

Mental improvement can conquer the feelings of inadequacy that many teens face and we can help. Prestige is acquired when your identity is revealed through your views, and we can help others achieve this. Mediocrity will never make it to the top and our goal is to put teens on top with knowledge. This is what we could help classmates achieve if we all take this class.

BreAnna invited me to her house next week so we can have a chance to talk about things for the philosophy class with our friends as a group. I'm so excited about seeing everyone. This is the first time BreAnna has ever had a get-together at her house. First thing she let me know is that Jake is still the most wonderful thing that has ever happened to her and in the same breath thanked me for introducing her to him. She let me know that they are staying true to the purity rings they are wearing. She let me know that God's ways are higher than our ways and by postponing sexual activity you are protecting your physical health and keeping your self-respect intact. You don't have to act on your sexual desire. It is good to know she is practicing self-control.

I let BreAnna know that I met someone special in Florida this summer. I told her the whole story. BreAnna was excited for me. She let me know it just gets better and better as long as you continue to obey God's rules. God's rules keep things simple, without guilt or pressure. Just don't do something you can't take back. Sounds like good advice from someone who has been in a relationship for several months now. BreAnna is a winner as far as relationships with the opposite sex goes, and advice from her is something I will value.

The next week was very restful. Mom and Dad went back to work and I spent my days reading a novel written for teens. I love to read; it keeps my mind sharp and brings me joy. A good author can make you feel the emotions of the characters in the stories.

Jeff emailed me every day to let me know what was going on in his world. Mostly it was about football practice. It has taken a lot of energy out of him and it showed in his emails. He didn't realize how out of shape he was until the coach pushed him past his limits. Jeff is spending a lot of time in the hot tub trying to loosen up his newly developed muscles. From the way he is talking, his movement is somewhat restricted due to soreness, but he has gained enormous muscular strength.

Jeff's brother requested Cloie's email address and now they are communicating on a regular basis. Since Matt also plays football, Cloie gets to hear about how sore he is from practice also. We get a kick out of sharing their, "poor me" hot tub stories. Sounds like the saying, "No pain, no gain," has a real meaning for these two.

I was chatting with Jeff one night on the webcam and as he was talking to me my mind was in such a whirl that I couldn't think straight at the sight of his dazzling eyes, and the magnificence of his sparkling smile that left me goose-pimply. I had to ask him to repeat himself because I hadn't heard a word he'd said.

Jeff said, "Chelsea, what's wrong with you today? You seem to be in a daze!"

I said, "Oh, well I got a sort of buzz, like a honeybee when I saw you and I couldn't focus." A really big smile came across his face. He knew my heart was his.

Jeff said, "You know I feel the same way. I never thought of the feeling as a honeybee but that was a pretty good description of the feeling. Where did you come up with such a vision?"

I replied, "We have beehives from which we harvest honey for our use, and we sell the rest for our vacation money. If it weren't for the honeybees, we would never have met. I go to the beehives on a regular basis and thank them for being instrumental in our friendship. When good things happen to me in life, I always give thanks to whatever was responsible for my good fortune. My dad taught me this very early in life. Dad gathers the honey from the beehives and always thanks the bees for their hard work. I now can appreciate their labor on the same level as my dad does. It is just more heart-felt now."

It's amazing how I just pour my heart's joy out to Jeff without hesitation. He brings out the best in me.

Jeff said, "Next time you thank the beehive, thank them for me also. Not a single soul on this earth has ever made me feel like you do. When you left Florida, I drew your name in the sand at least 100 times. I had to do something with my feelings. Drawing your name in the sand was somehow fulfilling. It was as if you were still there with me."

I said, "That's so sweet of you to tell me what is going on in your heart, for I'm feeling the same thing. You are the first person I've ever had a crush on and it's wonderful. I have tons of energy and just can't quit singing. On top of all this, I'm so glad you are such a good person. That is the most important thing to me. I know a lot of good guys, but never had any feelings for them in the form of a crush. I was afraid I might someday wind up with a bum or a bad guy, or maybe go through life with only friends. I'm so glad we share the same feelings."

With the exchange of all the goodness life has to offer, we said our goodnights and I turned off the computer.

BreAnna called me early in the morning to see if I would come to her house and help her get ready for the back to school party. It felt so good to be needed and I jumped on the chance to help. I agreed to spend the night and take her shopping in the morning for snacks.

When I pulled up to BreAnna's house, she came running out to see my new Mustang. She did a full circle around the car and let me know how hot I looked pulling into her driveway. We gave each other a hug and went into her house to start making a list of things for the party. First thing on the list is hamburger meat, and second are sesame seed buns. BreAnna is going all out with a full meal. She likes grilling outside and takes great pride in seasoning the meat with her special blend of spices and herbs she put together to enhance the flavor. Next on the list are all the garnishes to add extra flavor and color. Dill pickles served whole and sliced is my favorite part of a hamburger. I like the crunch. Lettuce and tomatoes are a must for burgers. White and yellow cheeses add variety. Mustard and mayonnaise are another choice we decided to give the guests. I suggested we get red onions and white onions for another choice.

That takes care of the burgers, and now it's time for the side dishes. Homemade French fries with the peelings left on is another favorite of mine. If the potato is sliced very thin and brushed with oil, we can put them in foil and grill them next to the burgers. The same can be done with yellow and green squash. You can pick them up with your fingers to eat. I brought tealeaves and honey to sweeten the drinks with. For dessert we agreed on cubed cantaloupe and watermelon. Now that the list was complete, it's time to talk about boys.

BreAnna has been dating Jake the genius for about seven months now and they seem to still be going strong on their feelings for one another. I have yet to mention I have a major crush on Jeff to BreAnna. I want to know what is going on in her world before I spring the news of my new guy. So in a very casual way I asked what all she did this summer. She jumped on the opportunity to start talking about the love of her life.

It started like this, "You know Chelsea, when two people are right for each other things just get better and better. We both want to make the other happy and that is a beautiful thing. It's like being with your best friend only with romance tied around the two of you. It is great to know this kind of happiness," BreAnna said.

I replied, "I'm so happy for you. Did the two of you get to spend much time together this summer?"

BreAnna went on to say, "As a matter of fact, we spent a great deal of time together. We both got on at Harjo's new and used guitar store. We work three days a week, eight hours a day. We go out every Saturday night either to a movie or out to eat or just to do something fun."

It is great to hear my two best friends are having the time of their lives. Now that Jeff is in my life, I understand how BreAnna and Jake feel. I understand how they can get lost into each other's world and be oblivious to everything else going on around them. You just get lost in each other when you have a major mutual crush. It's as if Jeff opened my eyes to the reality of what happens when two people who are right for each other become lost in their thoughts of one another. We are on each other's minds all the time. I guess it's time to share my summer with BreAnna now that she has brought me up to speed with what has happened in her world.

"BreAnna, I met someone this summer who has become very special to me. We just click. His name is Jeff and he lives in Texas. We met on the beach in Florida while I was on vacation. It was crush at first sight. I thought he would see me as not in his league because he is so good looking but when he looked slightly sheepish as he came near me, I then knew we were in the same league at heart. What was happening to me inside was also happening to him. I now completely understand what you and Jake have. I was a little fidgety at first because these feelings I have for him were completely foreign, until he grabbed my hand and a spark went off between us. At that moment I knew we were meant for each other. We keep in contact over the Internet with the webcam. Next time you are over I'll introduce you to him via the Internet," I said.

BreAnna gave me a hug and expressed her happiness for me. It was getting late and we decided to get some shut-eye. The party was planned for Sunday evening and we were going to church early in the morning.

After church and Sunday school we went to the

grocery store with our list. BreAnna was so excited about her little get together. She had never had a party before and she wanted everything to be perfect. Before leaving the store she double-checked the list. We must make sure we have all the goodies for the burgers. I'm getting a little gaga myself thinking about seeing all our friends. They will be arriving in about two hours.

To take some of the pressure off BreAnna I started slicing the onions and washing the lettuce. BreAnna sliced the tomatoes and cubed the cantaloupe and watermelon. We wrapped all of the goodies and put them in the refrigerator so they would stay crisp. I made the tea and poured a couple of glasses so we could take a break before the guest started arriving. It felt good to relax.

The first guests to arrive are Sara and Kyle with Zack in the backseat. We all exchanged hugs as the excitement mounted. Next to arrive was Jake, and BreAnna let out a squeal at the sight of him. Then Angela and Brad pulled up in Brad's new red truck. My heart is pumping with excitement. I can't wait to hear what all they did with their summer vacations.

I made everybody a glass of tea while BreAnna fired up the gas grill and made the hamburger patties. She was taking great pride in the seasoning of the burgers and the smell was delightful. Before the burgers were ready to come off the grill, BreAnna asked us to all join hands so she could say grace over the meal.

It went like this, "Thank you, Lord, for this meal on the Lord's day, Sunday. Thank you for all the goodness that each of these friends give of themselves. Keep us safe under the wings of the Holy Spirit. Amen."

Everyone began filling their plates and taking a seat. BreAnna's special seasoning is a hit. Everyone is bragging on the flavor and BreAnna is beaming. She is a perfect host.

After everyone finished his or her burger, BreAnna

said, "Let me have your attention. The underlying purpose of this gathering was to see what everyone did with their summer, and to let you know our school is offering a class about philosophies. If we all took the same class, I want to know what subject would you choose for your philosophy? This can start with me. I got a part time job at Harjo's used and new guitar store. The subject of true love and pursuit of wisdom by intellectual investigation and moral self-discipline will suit me. With that bit of information, let us hear what Jake has to say."

Jake said, "I also worked part time at Harjo's, and bought one of their guitars and currently I'm taking lessons. The subject that I would choose is to analyze and critique the fundamental beliefs of politics as they come to be conceptualized and formulated. Sara, how about you going next."

Sara said, "My passion is to have 'Peace on Earth,' and the only way to accomplish this is through freedom. Repressive measures are the cause of most wars, in my opinion. Since I am an only child, this summer I became a big sister for a set of twins who lost their parents in a car accident. Their names are Amy and Eva, and it is the most fulfilling thing to happen to me in my entire life. Let's hear what Kyle did this summer."

Kyle said, "Seeing how I will be going to a different high school, I'll go right to what my summer consisted of. New York is where I spent my summer. That's right, I went to summer school with a group of gifted music composers. I gained new perspectives, which made possible a new subjective evaluation of relative significance to my body of work. I'm one step closer to world peace through music. What did Angela do this summer?"

Angela said, "My grandparents put in a huge garden this summer and I helped maintain it by watering it daily and removing weeds during the day. In the evenings we sold our produce on the side of the road under a tarp. We had a lot of regular customers that we got to know on a personal basis. It was truly a wholesome feeling to share the work, the rewards, and the stories from the customers. The subject that suits me for the philosophies class is the importance of ethics. It is my opinion that ethics go hand in hand with respect of others and respect for yourself. They are guidelines that represent the right thing to do. Let's see what Brad has to offer."

Brad said, "I went to summer school because I failed English. This is not easy for me to acknowledge or admit to a weakness when I am among all of you geniuses, but it is a fact. I have problems in the learning department. However, a major improvement has taken place this summer. I made a B in English. The one on one study of the king's language made a real difference for me. For the philosophies class I will stick to something I truly do excel at, sports. This is something I totally understand, brute strength. With all that information about my weaknesses and strengths, let's move on to Zack."

Zack said, "Sorry about summer school Brad, but glad for your B and your passing. This summer I learned about a new way to catch a fish. It is called noodling. This is where you haphazardly put your hand into an unknown hole in the side of a riverbank or lake. You feel around looking for a catfish and when you find this fish you put your hand in either its mouth or in its gill and pull it out of the water and onto the bank. I pulled fish out that were longer than my arm! I filled my parents' freezer with catfish. It will last us all winter. The subject that would most suit me for the philosophies class is survival of the fittest. I would discuss natural selection, which is the struggle in which only those organisms best adapted to existing conditions survive. I think it's time to find out what's up with Chelsea."

I began with, "I had a wonderful two week vacation in Florida. I met a great group of young people who are committed to becoming centenarians, people who live to be 100 years old or older. To achieve this, they are committed to eating healthy foods and exercising regularly. To keep their minds sharp they draw straws everyday for who has to share a challenging new word that all must commit to memory. We should adopt this game because words have power. What I have chosen for a subject in the philosophies class is the power of friendship. It has made the biggest changes in my life and I want to share that power. By the way, it's good to see all of you again."

The party was low-key but it was a blast. It was great to see everyone and I'm excited about all of us taking philosophies together. It makes school way more fun when you share class with friends.

Chapter 5
Jeff's Accident

School starts in a couple of days and I'm going shopping for some new clothes. I've grown taller over the summer and my jeans are too short. I will salvage what I can of them by cutting them off right below the knee and then rolling them up above the knee. My skirts are a little shorter now that I have grown, but they still fit well enough for the moment. Most of my tops are stretchy so they actually look better this year than last since I fill them out more now. I gained seven pounds over the summer and it all went in the right places. During summer vacation in Florida I purchased two new shirts that were a couple sizes too big so that I could use them as cover-ups over my swimsuit. I will put a belt around my waist and they will look great with new jeans. I'm finding ways to save money because the cost of gasoline is going up and I am going to have to pay for car insurance, which is due in six months. There is a lot of responsibility that comes with driving a car.

The mall is crowded with people. I guess everyone is shopping for school clothes. I found a really neat store that had jeans that were stretchy. I will be able to wear these all year, even if I gain more weight. One pair has the front faded out and the other pair has worn spots on the knee. They look really stylish. I would buy every pair of jeans in this store if my pocketbook would allow it. I like this store so much that I put in an application for a part time sales position. The owner hired me to work three days a week after school, four hours a day at eight dollars an hour. With my new job and my allowance for helping around the house, I should be in pretty good shape.

When I got home from the mall I decided to try on my new jeans with one of the shirts I got in Florida and the seashell necklace Jeff gave me. They all look great together. The seashell got me thinking about Jeff so I turned on the computer and sent him a message. Jeff must have been on the computer because he answered immediately. He has instant messaging, which tells you when you have mail. We turned on our webcams and Jeff said, "Nice necklace, it looks great on you. It reminds me of that day on the beach when I gave it to you. Is that the same dental floss that you put through the hole and tied into a bow to make it look girly? I can see that it is. I remember everything about you, the way your hair smelled, the big smile on your face every time you looked at me, and the twinkle in your eye when we played a game. That's the competitive nature in you. I know because I have that same twinkle. We are a lot alike, which is probably one thing that has drawn us to each other. I am online every night hoping to catch you. You look beautiful tonight."

I blushed and said, "If I do indeed look beautiful its because the feeling that you give me is shining through. When you cross my mind I just start smiling, just like when we were in Florida. You just have that effect on me. I did dress just for you tonight with my new jeans and t-shirt and the necklace you gave me on the beach. So glad you noticed everything. You pop into my mind all the time for no reason. I don't try to make you become part of my thoughts, it just happens. I have no control over you."

Jeff replied, "That is just the way it is supposed to be. I just hope it continues to happen to you. As long as your mind has thoughts of me, I have a good chance of being with you in the future. But if for some reason you forget about me, I will always cherish the times we have shared together. I am aware of how difficult this relationship could be due to the distance between us."

I said, "Don't think for a second that I will ever forget about you. No one has ever awoken my body and mind like you have. I am around tons of guys all the time, but they are only friends. You are completely different than anyone I have ever met on this earth."

Jeff smiled and said, "That's nice to know. I feel the same way about you. My brother Matt is already falling for your sister, you know. She is all he can talk about. He is even worse than me, and I didn't even know that was possible. He's just all sappy. Whenever he is able to finally see her in person and hold her hand he will probably go crazy with excitement. That is what kind of shape he is in. I think it is funny to catch him talking to her online. She has him wrapped around her finger. You don't need to tell her that, we can just keep that between us."

We talked for another couple of hours and then said our goodnights. Our little chats give me more pleasure than I can put into words. It is a constant vibe and then some. It is the "then some" that I can't put into words.

It is exciting to know my sister has Matt's undivided attention. It would be really neat if Matt and Cloie got together and then someday got married. That would mean Jeff would always be in my life. I refuse to think about marriage myself, since I am only sixteen and in the middle of my first crush.

The next morning will be my last day of summer vacation and I plan to spend it swimming in the pond and playing with Bam. I packed a peanut butter and black currant jelly sandwich, a fruit bar, and jug of ice water. This will be a great day to spend at the pond for the water is warm from the summer days on top and cool down deep from the spring that feeds it. With my big floppy hat, sunglasses, towel and a tube, off I go. Bam is waiting at the backdoor so I grab a handful of jellybeans, give her one and put the rest in my pocket. Bam is right beside me all the way, looking at me with those big brown eyes, begging for another jelly bean, so I give her another. As we arrive at the pond the birds are singing as if they are a symphony orchestra composed of strings, wind, and percussion sections, designed for playing a song just for me. As I near the pond a frog jumps in and makes a big splash. This place is truly what peace on earth looks like. A squirrel stands on his hind legs and chatters at me as if I should understand what he is saying, then turns and runs off into the woods. A big yellow butterfly is going from one wild flower to another collecting nectar to give his glorious wings more brilliant colors. The combination of these things is what is making this a happy place in my life.

My favorite way to get into the water is to swing out on the rope and splash into the deepest part of the pond. It wakes up all of my senses as I go from warm to what feels like an icebox at the bottom of the pond. It is a lot of different feelings in a short amount of time. As I rise to the top of the water, the light through my eyelids grows brighter and brighter until my head emerges from the water, and the brightness of the sun showers down on my face.

I swim across the pond a couple of times and then take a break. As I sit on the edge of the water, Bam steps next to me to take a drink and then looks me right in the eye. I give her a scratch behind the ear and she leans into the scratch as if to say, "Please don't stop."

It is time to blow up my tube so I can soak up some Vitamin D, or sunshine as some call it. The warm morning sun on my face calms my whole body and it is as if I am half awake and half asleep. The sun coming through the trees reflects off the leaves giving a twinkling effect. As I lay on my float I say to myself, this is truly a happy place.

When I returned to my home it was time to take an outdoor shower because pond water has organisms in it. As I dry my hair, my cell phone begins to ring. I answer it and it is Cloie on the other end. I could tell something was wrong by the way she was talking.

She said, "Hey little sister, Matt just phoned me and Jeff has had an accident. During football practice, his helmet cracked when he took a hit and he suffered a concussion, which caused injury to the soft structure of his brain. He is in the hospital and Matt wanted me to tell you. He is unconscious, currently unable to think or feel. The doctors' diagnosis is that he is temporarily in a coma, but he should wake up in time. Chelsea? Chelsea, are you okay?"

I leaned against the wall to keep from falling. My head felt light as a feather as I slid down the wall and sat on my heels to keep from fainting. The news was devastating and tears poured down my face. I was unable to speak because of the lump in my throat.

Somehow, Cloie sensed that I was unable to speak and she just said, "Chelsea, he will be alright. I just know that he will. I know you are unable to speak but I feel your pain. I am here for you and I want you to lean on me for support when you need it. I know I am on the other side of the world, but you can pick up the phone or turn on the computer any time, night or day, and I will answer. I hear your silence and know why you can't find the words to speak. You don't need to say anything; you can just hang up the phone. I will be praying for Jeff. Call me if you need me."

With that, I hung up the phone, for I could not even find the words to say goodbye. I put my hands on my head to keep it from exploding with all of the emotions and thoughts whirling around inside of it. How could this happen to such a wonderful human being? He has a heart of gold and was doing so much good for teens. I care so much for him and can't stand to think of him in pain.

I made my way to my bed and lay down, grabbed a pillow and hugged it tight. Sorrow and fear filled my heart. What if Jeff never recovers and remains in this state of existence, unable to awake for the rest of his life? These fears consumed my thoughts. Helplessness describes this situation best.

My mom knocked on the door and said, "Chelsea, are you okay?"

I must have dozed off to sleep because of all the stress. The door opened and Mom came in with two glasses of iced tea. She set them down on the dresser and gave me a hug. We held each other in silence, unable to speak.

The family is giving their full support, and it is truly appreciated, however one must live with their own pain. The ability to cure the emotional imbalance is a gift from God. One must be free from anxiety and other negative forces. They never force themselves on others in order to prove themselves. It takes a lot of energy out of the person who heals the emotionally sick person. They must be selfless in order to have the gift of healing. That person must be a servant of God to be able to reach their full potential. My mom has all these traits and eventually I know she will reach me, but for now I must learn to deal with the pain.

It has been two weeks and Jeff has yet to wake. I pray day and night for his recovery and this helps as much as anything. Mom always gives me a big hug before bedtime and it is appreciated. She feels the pain and so wants to remove it.

God's plan is that healing takes place through prayer. If one is not healed it is still God's plan. It must be God's will for a person to be healed. Chronic illness must be prayed for daily for months and in some cases years. Prayer must be soaked up like a sponge to help the natural recuperative forces in the body to get to work. I have prayer on my breath for Jeff constantly.

My friends at school had no idea I cared so much for Jeff. I am sort of private about my feelings as a general rule, but right now there is no way to hide my emotions. I'm trying to put on a front but am not doing a very good job. Anyway, not with those who know me. At my part-time job things are going great though because people don't know my personality yet so they cannot perceive any of my feelings. However, family and friends know the pain I am feeling and see it clearly.

I am going to search for solutions to my pain and let God guide me through this journey. My need to talk to Jeff has me calling his family to see if they will put the phone to Jeff's ear so that I can speak the words of encouragement that are on my heart. I want to tell him what is going on with me as I normally would, even if he cannot respond. Jeff's mother agreed to call me on a Sunday and hold the phone to Jeff's ear so that I could speak to him.

I said, "Hi Jeff, this is Chelsea. My heart is bleeding with sorrow for you every day. You must do everything you can to come back to everyone who loves you. I miss you so much that it is unbearable. Please give any kind of sign that you understand what I am saying. Your mother is holding the phone to your ear so that I can talk to you, and let you know that my life is so much better when you are in it. You are the first guy that I have ever had a crush on and no matter what the future brings you will have a special place in my heart forever. My heart is breaking that you can't respond to me. I believe in the healing power of music and I am going to ask your mom to play my favorite song at least twice a week so when you wake up we can talk about how many times you heard that song. Your mom is probably getting tired of holding the phone so I will say my goodbyes. I will keep you in my prayers and my heart."

It was so nice of Jeff's mom to do that for me. She continued to do so once a week. It took a lot of the grief from my heart even though Jeff never responded in any way. I was able to release some of my feeling though and in my heart I knew it was doing both of us a lot of good.

It has been four weeks now since Jeff's concussion. He is not responding to any stimulus the doctors administrate. However, he does have brain waves and the doctors still think he could snap out of the coma at any time. I keep having this overwhelming need to hold Jeff's hand so that I can see if the vibe we shared is still there. I so want to touch him.

When Mom came through the door after work, I told her that Jeff didn't respond to the telephone connection again. She gave me a hug and let me know how sorry she was.

I said, "If only I could hold his hand, so I could know if he could feel my touch. Sometimes I think if he could only feel my touch he might just wake up. The only way I will ever know is if I go there and grab his hand and feel the connection we have. Jeff's mom said she would fly me down if I wanted. I guess that means Jeff told her how he feels about me. She said I could stay in his room so it won't cost much. Matt lives on campus and Ed lives with his friend. I am sure everything will be fine. I will fly out on Friday night and get back home on Sunday morning. Please, Mom, this is something I really need to do."

Mom called Jeff's mother and they agreed to split the expenses. Both agree that everyone would benefit from the outcome no matter what it is. The best outcome would be that Jeff would open his eyes, but if he doesn't then we can all know we did everything possible to get him to wake up. If it's all you can do then it's all you can do.

I packed my bags as soon as I got home and Mom took me to the airport. It is only a 45-minute flight and Jeff's mother has a sign saying, "Here I am, Chelsea."   When I saw the sign after getting off the plane, I approached her and said, "Hi, I am Chelsea Songbird."

Jeff's mother gave me a hug and said, "You are just as pretty as Jeff said you were." She gave me a very warm welcome. We went straight to the hospital. Jeff's dad was waiting for us in Jeff's room and had a big smile on his face when we walked through the door.

He said, "You must be Chelsea. My son spoke very highly of you when he was awake. We are so pleased to meet you. I see the Cherokee in you very clearly."

I said, "Yes, I am very proud of my Native American heritage and very pleased to meet you as well."

When I looked at Jeff he just looked like he was sleeping. He looked so peaceful that I felt a little better about the situation immediately. He has his loving family around him and I see no pain in his face. Jeff's dad started telling me about his three sons all playing football. He himself played when he was in high school. It is a family tradition. The unfortunate accident of the helmet breaking has changed their lives. The helmet was Ed's from when he played football in high school. Apparently it was defective, but no one had known this. I suggested the family try having an intervention by letting Ed know how much he was worth to them. As a matter of fact, the one thing Jeff wished he could do was bring Ed out of his drug-induced stupor. I could be a witness of Jeff's greatest wish if they wanted me to express it to Ed. The family agreed it would be worth a try. I am already here and willing to participate. If they can get Ed to agree to come talk then it will happen.

I had time to get to know Jeff's parents and I am hoping he is hearing my voice as we talk. Soon his parents will leave the room though and Jeff and I will have a few moments together. Not just yet though because his parents still want to know more about me. I showed them the shell around my neck that Jeff found for me on the beach in Florida. They each picked it up and then laid it back on my chest. I asked if when I go home could Jeff's mother wear it until Jeff wakes up. A tear rolled off her cheek and she said, "I will be honored."

The time has come for being alone with Jeff. My heart is stuck in my throat. Will Jeff respond? Before I can muster up the guts to touch his hand, I will have a one-way conversation.

I began saying, "Jeff, if you can hear me, you know I am here. Your mom and my mom paid for me to fly down here and see you. I am staying with your parents, but I came straight from the airport to here so I haven't been to your house yet. You look great. It is so good to see you. I am here to hold your hand and see if we can feel the vibe that we felt last time our hands touched. I think if you have enough familiar things around you, it might help you wake up. Jeff, I am going to hold your hand now."

As I picked up Jeff's hand, a tear rolled down my cheek and dripped off my chin. There is no feeling. I take his hand to my cheek and kiss the back of it.

I told Jeff, "I am so sorry, but I can feel nothing. My heart is breaking in two." I sat in total silence, absent of any sound, not even a whimper. When Jeff's parents entered the room, they knew the outcome of my attempt. No one spoke a word on the way home to Jeff's house.

His mother showed me Jeff's room and said, "There is food in the refrigerator if you are hungry. I am going to bed, so I will see you in the morning." I was still at a loss for words so I just nodded my head.

Morning started with pancakes with blueberries on top.

"Jeff told me you like honey, so I warmed some up for your pancakes," Jeff's mother said. Breakfast gave me the energy I needed, for I was unable to eat anything the night before.

The day will be filled with Jeff's family. His brothers will be joining us at the hospital today. I've met Matt via the computer, so Ed is the only member of the family I haven't met yet. I am nervous to see what Ed will be like. Jeff told me Ed has lost his soul and there is nothing he wanted more than for Ed to reclaim it and put his drugs away and be part of his family once again. Today Ed will be asked to participate in an intervention to his drug addiction. I will do all I possibly can to get Ed to clean up his act.

When we got to the hospital, Matt and Ed were already there. Matt grabbed me and gave me a hug and while he was hugging me he introduced me to Ed. I shook Ed's hand and told him how much Jeff loved him and talked about him. Ed looked down at the floor as I mentioned Jeff's name. Jeff's mom and dad wanted to do an intervention with Ed but they don't want him to know that it is happening. I suggested we hold hands around Jeff's bed and each say a prayer.

When it came to my turn, I said, "Dear Lord, we all so want Jeff to wake up, but we put him into your hands. Jeff loves his family and has showed me concern for his brother Ed. Ed has abandoned his family and Jeff is missing his big brother. Jeff told me that even when Ed is at the house, his mind is not present. Please Lord, bring Ed back to Jeff's family."

Ed looked ashamed as I spoke, and finally looked at Jeff and said, "Little brother, it should be me laying there instead of you. It was my helmet that put you in this bed, and I am so sorry." About that time, we dropped hands and Ed's father grabbed him and gave him a hug.

They both sobbed for a while, then dried their eyes and their dad began saying, "Jeff's not the only one who wants you back. Your whole family misses you." This is the beginning of the great intervention. Their mother is the one who finally found the courage to put forth the question of whether Ed would be willing to get help if everyone gave him their support. Ed started saying that he didn't want to get everyone's hopes up because he wasn't sure he could do it.

He was trying to get out of it when I said, "Please, just try. It would be such a beautiful gift to Jeff if when he wakes up you were a viable part of the family again. He was wearing your helmet because he misses his brother." Ed just put his hands around his head and was silent.

Sunday came too soon for me. Jeff's mother is taking me to the hospital to be with Jeff for a while before I fly home. Did I really think he would react to my touch or did I really just need to see him? It is a little of both I think. When we got to the hospital, Jeff's mother dropped me off so that I could spend some time alone with him. The first thing I told Jeff was that I thought Ed wanted to quit doing drugs and that now he now has a reason to stop. He wants his little brother to wake up and see that he is part of the family again. The second thing I said was that I miss talking to him and that the crush I have on him is as strong as ever. As I hold Jeff's hand, I feel nothing. It is truly one of the saddest days of my life.

The trip home is going by fast. Only 45 minutes and I am back in Oklahoma.   My mom picked me up from the airport and the first thing she said was, "There's my baby girl." She is being so sweet and supportive through this whole nightmare. Jeff lay in that bed motionless, not responding to my touch, not even a twitch. This has crushed my soul. The question now is if Jeff never wakes up, will I be able to move on with my life? I am so blessed to have a great family, friends, and all the physical things like a great home to live in, a new car and a great school. Yet a dark cloud follows me around since Jeff's accident. I must accept the fact that he may never wake up.

Chapter 6
Philosophies

The class all my friends enrolled in called Philosophies has become a huge blessing in my life. The dark cloud that follows me around since Jeff's accident is nowhere in sight while this class is in session. Depression for me is a state of mind. I can control it at this point if I choose to. My condition is not a physical condition as some forms of depression are. Mine is caused by a series of events, which I have no control over. I have suffered a great loss and now must accept whatever outcome the future holds for Jeff. I must choose to either not think of Jeff so often or to think about him in a positive way. It will be a little of both.

Our teacher's name is Mr. Holt and he allows us to pick the topic we want to discuss in class. The first person in class to discuss their philosophy was BreAnna. She started out like this: "I want to discuss true love and the pursuit of wisdom by intellectual investigation and moral self-discipline. In my analysis of the words 'true love' I have come to the understanding that these two words are equal to, which means being the same in value, the word happiness. Don't confuse the overwhelming sexual feelings that emerge in adolescence with true love. Your body is a precious gift so you shouldn't allow anyone to think they are entitled to use your body for their selfish gratification.

True love does not make you a slave of animal passion. It seems to take an eternity of time to understand the mysterious voices in one's own head, crying out to please the flesh. There are two forces in the universe, one belonging to the devil and the other to God. Who will you choose to let dominate your actions?

It is God's wish that you choose a mate for life. Some people go into marriage with the idea that if it doesn't work out we can always get a divorce. They are setting themselves up for failure before they even get started. Marriage is a lifelong commitment to a monogamous relationship that will bring joy to your hearts for as long as you both shall live. If you are fortunate enough to be virgins when you marry, you are giving each other the gift of true love that is unblemished, the way God meant for marriage to begin. However, if a snake charmed you into sin, you can ask God to forgive you and he will. Forgiveness is a gift from God.

Abstinence results in self-pride. It is a tool used by most teens to resist the pressure to be sexually active. Teens can keep their human dignity by practicing abstinence and selflessness. Saying no to sex is an option.

If teens can postpone sexual encounters until they get married, their chance of having a successful relationship for a lifetime increases. To achieve this they must set sexual limits and use self-control. Peer pressure is the biggest reason teens have sexual relations. Abstinence is the only sure way for protection.

In order to experience the ultimate sexual act to its fullest, one must be free of fear of contracting a disease or getting pregnant. When a couple is married they no longer hold back physically or emotionally, they can give themselves completely to each other.

Teen sex is not safe. It is immoral and in most cases

it is illegal. The male and female very often have different reasons for having sexual relations. Sex should never be used as a test for one's love. If you are being sent a subliminal message, which is something used to stimulate below the threshold of conscious perception, don't let it affect you. This is one of the devil's most powerful tools. When you feel this happening to you, look at every outcome the message can produce. Will the outcome affect your happiness in the long run?

If you want to be a virgin on your wedding night, avoid foreplay that leads to sexual arousal, because at that point it is difficult to stop. Saying no and walking away shows how strong you are. Sex is one of the deepest commitments one human can make to another. Cherish it on your wedding night. If you hold onto your virginity until your wedding night you will be giving your mate the greatest gift possible. Another gift that you will be giving yourself is self-respect that comes with giving your virginity on your wedding night.

To sum up, true love equals happiness. I believe sexuality is nothing to be ashamed of. It is a gift from God to be enjoyed by married couples. In a sexual moment we totally lose ourselves and become one in the eyes of God and he will bless our union. Sexual pleasure within marriage is God's gift to mankind, and we are allowed the feelings of sexual pleasure and God encourages us to use them. God will give us the wisdom to make the right choices in life if we just ask. With the right choices comes true love which equals happiness."

Mr. Holt said, "Well done, BreAnna. If more young people followed your philosophy the world would be a better place. With values like this the children of the future would be less likely to get into trouble. Broken homes make it more difficult for young people. We have time for one more presentation. How about you, Jake? Are you prepared?"

"Yes I am, and my philosophy will be on politics and

the importance of honesty for those who hold an office.

At the core of mankind, there is a need to protect their family. When Americans go to the polls to vote, this is what is in the back of their minds as they cast their vote. It would be a travesty if the person they put in office turned out to be dishonest. This is why the record of politicians is so important. Their record reflects their beliefs. They cannot hide from their record; it is public for anyone to see.

I'm going to use our penal code, the body of laws pertaining to crimes and offense and the penalties for their commission, as examples of what should be changed by our politicians in today's times.

Our jails are so full we have to release criminals before their full sentence, punishment to be inflicted, is served. Let's say someone is sentenced to 20 years but they are let out after serving only 10 years because of overcrowding. The governor of a state can pardon a criminal, so you need to know if he or she is soft on crime. There are some crimes that criminals should never be released early from and on the other hand there are crimes which people should never be sent to prison for. The non-violent crimes could be treated differently. These people could be restricted from leaving their home by putting an ankle bracelet around their leg and having the perimeter, the outer limits of their home, have a laser beam that sets off an alarm whenever they step outside of the boundaries. It could be an alarm that the neighbors can hear so they can be warned that the convict has violated his house arrest. A GPS locator could be inside of this ankle bracelet so the prisoner could be located no matter where they go. An alarm would be sent to the police station immediately if he violates the arrangement.

I want to take this a step further and offer good citizens the opportunity to house these non-violent prisoners for at least $25,000 a year. The prison system in many states charges $40,000 a year to house prisoners. This would be a tremendous amount of money to save for the taxpayers in these states.

Bad things can happen to young people who go to prison. In many cases, they come out of prison more violent than they were before they went in. In my opinion, any prisoner who is housed in a good citizen's house will be a better person because of the influence of the good citizens they stayed with. This will give income to people who make house payments and save taxpayers large sums of money.

Hard core criminals should be housed in penitentiaries on large pieces of land where they can till the soil and plant the food they consume. There should be enough vegetables and fruits that they can also can fruit in jars for the winter. Cattle, hogs and chickens should be fed and watered by the inmates for their meat. There is no reason why taxpayers should pay for criminals' food.

This could all be accomplished with the right politicians in office. Everyone old enough to vote should know who their legislators are, for they are the ones who create and enact laws. With honest politicians, laws can be made that reduce state taxes, instead of raising them to house criminals."

"That was very impressive Jake. Knowing whom you are voting for is very important to your future. Freedom in this country came at the price of many lives. We must protect our freedom with our vote. Jake, that was a magnificent presentation that shows the power that votes have to change things for the better," Mr. Holt said.

That was all for today and my friends did a great job of opening the eyes of the philosophy class of students. After all, we are the future of this great country and we need to protect our freedoms. We need to make sure our taxes are spent on things that are necessary to run our states and our country.

BreAnna did a great job on true love and saving your

body for your future husband, and for the guys, their future wives. She is right on target about the divorce rate being so high because of the mindset, "If it doesn't work out we can just get a divorce."

The next day came before I knew it. Mr. Holt asked for volunteers and Sara raised her hand.

She started out with, "My philosophy paper is on the topic of peace on earth. With the Internet being a worldwide networking tool, peace on earth could be achieved. People have always looked for popular things to do, and if peace became popular among our youth, it could be a new way of life worldwide. It is difficult to change the minds of older people, so the world will have to grow into the concept of world peace. I have a friend named Kyle who goes to a private school and he is working on music that has subliminal messages, which are messages sent below the threshold of conscious perception, and he thinks his music will start the peace on earth movement.

People around the world can be educated on how to elect a good leader for their country. If the wrong leaders are elected, the world could end because of access to nuclear powered weapons in the world. It is more important for countries to elect leaders who can work for the world as a whole than any other time in the history of our existence. Education through the Internet can make this possible."

Mr. Holt said, "Sara, your presentation was short but very powerful. It was to the point and gave a solution for the problem. Good job. Do we have a volunteer to go next?" Zack raised his hand and Mr. Holt nodded his approval.

Zack said, "Survival of the fittest is what my philosophy paper is about. Strength comes in many packages, whether physical, mental, or moral strengths. They will be my topics. The old saying, "only the strong survive," has a lot of meaning to me. If a natural disaster or a man-caused disaster occurred, the people who were left would need the skills of how to hunt in order to feed themselves. This would require physical strength and know how to do it. The moral strength would come in the form of being able to share the meat with others. Hunting has become a lost art in the world we live in today. Many experts say if the world experienced a disaster we will go back in time to an age somewhat like the caveman days. The underlying reality is that mankind would have to develop new laws to fit the circumstances and use logical reasoning to rule the new world. New viewpoints would be presented for just staying alive and finding the next meal. Strength and endurance would be required, for it could be more than a day to find just one meal.

So, my question to you, class, is how many of you could have the strength to hunt down your next meal and the intelligence to even know how and where to find it?"

Mr. Holt clapped his hands and said, "It is true that hunting for our meals is becoming a lost art. If what Zack talked about today happened tomorrow, how many of you would survive? It is something to think about. We have time for one more presentation. Do we have any volunteers?"

I raised my hand and I was on my feet talking before I knew it.

"My philosophy is on the power of friendship. It is a life-changing experience to gain a friend that clicks with your personality. Friendship is powerful and can lift your spirits with just a simple conversation. When someone offers you their friendship, it should be treasured and never abused, for it can be taken away and never given back.

To be someone's friend you must make yourself warm-hearted and congenial to be around. This is necessary so people will want to get to know you. Making friends is not always easy, even for people who seem to be very popular. A friendship that could possibly be a lifelong relationship is hard to come by. You may have hundreds of acquaintances but only ten people who have the label of a true friend.

So many times friendships are lost because someone thinks they have been wronged. If you think you are about to do something wrong to a friend, chances are you might ruin that friendship. Because friendships can be so powerfully strong in the way that they bring you happiness, at the same time they can be fragile and easily broken because of just one betrayal, or what a friend perceives to be a betrayal.

People are complicated and if you value your friendship you will keep things simple. Putting expectations on a friend is the same as pressuring them and that stresses the relationship. This is why so many young people change friends throughout their school years: too many expectations.

When you find your true friends, and you will if you keep looking, it is a very powerful feeling. You gain a sense of security and you learn to be loyal without anyone demanding it of you. The sense of security makes you want to do right by your friends because you want their respect. My philosophy is to find your friend, always treat them right, and they will always be there for you and that is powerful."

Mr. Holt said, " Thank you, Chelsea, for your choice in subject. I personally have two friends that I have cherished for the past 25 years and they have a very powerful effect on my life. I challenge every student in this class to go out and make a new friend and follow Chelsea's philosophy on how to treat the relationship. That's all for today, see you tomorrow."

This is a great class and I am so happy all my friends are taking it together. We are having a blast. Brad and Angela will do their presentation on Monday and I can't wait to hear what subjects they chose.

The weekend is here and on Saturday night we are going roller-skating. Zack is picking me up at 7 p.m. and we are meeting all our friends.

When Zack pulled into the driveway I was sitting on the porch waiting for him.

He said, "Hop in, we have time for an ice cream cone. I was hoping you would be ready early. You know, Chelsea, I really enjoyed your presentation Friday on friendship. I so value our friendship. It is comfortable and I just really enjoy being with you. We are not the boyfriend/girlfriend type relationship yet I enjoy being with you more than my past girlfriends. We have fun."

I replied, "When I wrote my paper you were in the back of my mind the whole time. I always get a powerful feeling when I am with you and it is not just because of all those muscles."

He laughed and then we had our ice cream and talked for a while and then the subject of Jeff came up.

"How's that guy you met in Florida doing? Jeff, wasn't it?" he asked me.

I said, "Thanks for asking, but there has been no change. He could wake up at any moment though. I call once a week and his mom puts the phone up to his ear so that I can talk to him. The pain has lessened some only because I have been staying busy to keep my mind off the fact that he is in a coma. Jeff would want me to go on with life. He is just that kind of guy. Let's get in there and teach Angela how to skate."

Everyone already had their skates on and Angela had Brad on one side and Sara on the other holding her hand. I've been roller-skating for so many years I can't imagine how anyone that is sixteen years old doesn't know how to skate.

It's time to relieve Brad and Sara, so Zack and I get on each side of Angela. We took it slow and Angela was jerky trying to keep her balance. We took a couple of laps around the rink and Angela seemed to be keeping her balance so we turned her loose. Angela's legs looked like she was beginning to do the splits and next thing we knew she ran right into the wall and fell on her butt. We picked her up and took her to a booth to set down. She told us to go have some fun and that she would try again later.

The music was loud and the strobe lights were flashing in every direction. Brad was showing off by skating backwards and dancing at the same time. If the Olympic games had a roller skating competition, Brad could win for the United States. He's that good.

Angela was once again on her feet, or should I say on her skates, and this time BreAnna and Jake were holding her up. She's going faster now so we do have some improvement in the training of our friend. Angela looks a lot like a baby learning how to walk, unbalanced and uncertain. She really should have learned to skate when she was young; your butt is a lot closer to the ground and it doesn't hurt so much when you fall.

Kyle was showing off by skating on one foot and doing all kinds of foolish thing that finally caused him to fall flat on his face. We couldn't help but laugh at him. He got up, brushed himself off and took Angela by both hands. Her eyes got really big like she was trying to say, "Help! This guy is a train wreck and you're leaving me alone with him?" People can say a lot with their eyes.

We all decided to take a break, grab a bottled water and rest for a while. Because Zack had brought up Jeff to me when we were eating ice cream, Jeff was on my mind. During vacation we did all kinds of physical things like beach volleyball and surfing. Afterwards was the drawing of the straws. Someone draws the short straw and had to introduce a new word to be added to our vocabulary so we could be smarter. It's time for my friends to play this game.

I used toothpicks and only one out of the eight was short. Sara drew the short toothpick and her word was spontaneous, which means impulsive or unpremeditated. We all knew what the word meant but now we will use it when we have conversations. The word I chose when in Florida was 'fundamental', which is another word for basic, but it sounds better. If we keep playing the game, when we become adults we will sound very sophisticated and the way you talk helps you get the better jobs.

This was an opportunity for me to talk about Jeff. My friends were feeling my pain and encouraged me to deal with the situation.

I said, "Jeff would be proud that we are playing the game he made up to broaden our vocabulary. He has another game using the same technique of drawing the short toothpick, but it is for something to better our health so we can live to be centenarians, a person 100 years old or older, and still be in good health. Jeff drew the short straw and he told a story about how he had gone to the doctor because he keeps getting muscle cramps. The doctor told him to eat more bananas or pears. Jeff likes pears so he planted a pear tree and his mother cans them so he can have pears all year long. He also saves a ton of money because pears are expensive."

After telling the story I wiped my face because a tear had rolled down my cheek. I don't know how it happened because I was not crying. Somehow it just fell out my eye. Zack noticed and changed the subject by saying, "We have 30 minutes to skate until this place closes down."

On the way home Zack let me know that he would always be there for me. He told me to never hesitate to talk about Jeff because it will help to heal my heart.

Monday came and Mr. Holt once again asked for volunteers to share their philosophy with the class.

Angela raised her hand, and began, "I first started doing my paper on the importance of ethics, because they keep society in line, but my paper evolved into how the lack of ethics which is the main cause of gangs. Everybody wants control. Social ills will leave the underprivileged less privileged than ever and more susceptible to joining a gang. A gang leader will be able to force the less privileged into submission because it is easy to lose your way in life when you have nothing.

If you live in a poor neighborhood your child is at risk of joining a gang. Other factors that cause kids to join gangs are poor parenting, allowing delinquent behavior, and having traumatic events in one's past. Only about 15% of kids in a given neighborhood join gangs. Knowing the reasons why kids join can be a powerful tool in preventing the growth of gangs.

Low grades in school cause self-esteem problems and make kids targets for gang recruitment. With low grades come bad attitudes. Programs such as tutoring, counseling, and anger management can make a difference. Pain and anger go hand in hand and create a monster. The Internet has gangs growing and I expect that 15% to rise to 25% if this problem is not shown more attention.

Our youth need more places to go when their home life is so bad that they leave home and live on the streets. My philosophy is that if they have a place that is safe and warm with food provided, gangs will have a difficult time recruiting them. I come from a bad home life but thank God my grandparents took me in. If my grandparents had not taken me in I would have been living on the streets myself.

People give money for all kinds of charities and it is my opinion that our youth in this great country should be the ones people give money to. We need shelters that would be much like a private school where they learn and live so they don't wind up being a burden to themselves and to make the whole country safer in the future.

For those who want to get out of a gang, charity foundations could be set up to remove the tattoos that most gangs require. When you have a gang tattoo you are marked for life unless you have it removed.

Another way of dealing with gangs could be a gang for those who do good. Some youth just want to belong somewhere and to be something. If they had a gang to join that stood for everything good in life instead of the bad we could save those just looking to fit in somewhere. It is my opinion that by investing in our youth today we will have a safer and happier future."

Mr. Holt said, "Great choice to do your paper on. Gang violence is a threat to our freedom and is growing daily. I totally agree that most of our youth that join gangs are just looking for a place to fit in. Good job! Do we have any more volunteers?"

About that time Angela sat down and Brad raised his hand and went to the front of the class.

He said, "I chose sports as the subject for my philosophy paper and the impact they have worldwide. The Olympic games are a Pan-Hellenic Festival of athletic games and contests of dance and choral poetry, first held in 776 B.C. and celebrated at four-year intervals until A.D. 393 on the plain of the Olympian Zeus. Today, a modern international revival of athletic contests patterned after the Olympic games is held every four years. Their sporting events have a bigger effect of bringing people of the world together on friendly terms than anything I know of. If nations could challenge each other in different sporting events on a regular basis, bonds could be formed that would open communication between the nations to solve problems of the world. For example, golf is played so business people can get to know each other better and discuss business in an enjoyable environment. If leaders of different nations played golf while discussing problems on a regular basis, they could make more progress resolving differences, because they will get to know each other better and hopefully bond.

Golf is a sport that no matter what your size, you can compete on an even playing field. If they get upset at one another they can just hit the ball harder. My philosophy is to try bringing leaders of the world into a environment that could solve problems on a friendly basis."

Mr. Holt said, "Thank you Brad, I prefer golf over war myself. If you could prevent just one war the world would be a better place. That's all for today."

Chapter 7
Thanksgiving

It's now been four months since Jeff's accident and he has yet to wake up. His mother and I talk on a regular basis and she helps me deal with the situation. She is so grateful for my input for her son Ed during the intervention of his drug problem. Ed checked himself into a drug rehab center the next week and has completely recovered and is living with his parents until he feels strong enough mentally to live on his own. He found a whole new set of friends to keep the temptation for drugs out of his life. With his old set of friends drugs are a way of life and Ed knows he would fall right back into his old habit forming ways. He's just not strong enough to say no. Like he says, out of sight is out of mind.

Something good has come out of Jeff's tragedy for his family. Ed woke up to the fact that his drug addiction caused his family a great deal of pain and knew his recovery would be a gift for Jeff when he wakes up.

Cloie and Matt spend a lot of time on the Internet communicating their feelings for one another. I can feel Cloie's enthusiasm, when she talks about Matt. If I say so myself, his sheepish smile will get to your heart. It's just so sweet. Sometimes he emails me about his brother Ed's recovery. He thinks what I said to Ed was the main reason Ed went into rehab. Matt said to me, "When we pray for the sick, and drug addiction is a sickness, our current of energy is received by them if they allow it in. The energy will flow through their body and begin to heal them. God's wishes will be the end result of our prayers, and for Ed it was to be healed. Ed learned in rehab that the devil dwells in lust and drugs and steals your peace. If you turn your back on evil a whole new world will open for you.

You must look at the difference between mental problems which are psychological and those that are spiritual. Ed let his guard down and the devil entered his body. He was able to put the drugs down when he said no to the devil and asked the Holy Spirit to help him through this nightmare of drugs. If he hadn't confessed his problems it would have been much more difficult for him to get well. Ed had a great childhood and was very stable, but he just fell in with the wrong group of people. What started out as having fun with drugs became a habit that owned his life.

His mom said, "Chelsea, somehow you were able to reach Ed and we thank you from the bottom of our hearts. You were the answer to our prayers. God sent you to us."

I've always known that human beings have been given the talent to heal through prayer by God's mercy, but now I've seen the results. I'm being as patient as possible for results in Jeff's recovery, and I continue to pray at 7 p.m. every evening while Jeff's family prays at the exact same time for his eyes to open.

The thought that Jeff may die crosses my mind occasionally and I remember what my uncle told me on his deathbed, "When it's time for death we must accept God's will and pray for the strength to let go. No one escapes death, but death leads us to heaven, that which only comes through death." Those were very powerful words that helped me understand, sometimes we have to let go of the one's we love and let God have them. When my uncle died I remember I felt light as a feather, in a kind of swoon that was full of sweetness as I received the gift of Understanding. My blood still chilled though in my veins at the thought that Jeff might die. He's so young. My uncle had a full good life and letting go seemed natural. Jeff has so much unfinished business. My heart was beating like a bass drum at the thought of Jeff dying. I had to get up and go outside for some fresh air. Bam was at the back door and I gave her a hug. With that my mind came back to the reality that Jeff is still alive and I must continue to pray for him.

The doorbell rang and I went back inside to answer the door.

"Hi, Zack, come on in," I said.

Zack had a look that said, "Tell me what's wrong" as soon as he saw my face.

I said, "Nothing."

Zack was a trifle stubborn and said, "Tell me what's wrong right now."

I said, "Some bad thoughts of Jeff never waking up came across my mind and I freaked out."

Zack looked at me sympathetically but told me firmly, "Don't lose your faith, continue praying."

Things were quiet for a very long moment. Zack never talked to me in this tone and I knew not to say anything more about the subject. I asked him if he would like a cup of hot tea and he nodded yes. I asked what kind of tea would he like and he said, "Surprise me." Surprised he was for a taste of seven different tealeaves was what he got, blended together with just a smidgen of honey.

Zack said, "Wow, that's really good. What I came by for, Chelsea, was to see if you wanted to go turkey hunting with Mom, Dad and yours truly. Mom said she would get a bird for your family, and you know dad has to put a bird on his family's table every year. Me and you are going along to pick which bird they shoot."

I said, "Let me call my dad and let him know where I'm going."

It was okay with Dad so I went upstairs to put on my camouflage outfit so I could appear to be part of the natural surroundings so the birds could not see me. Zack went out the back door to give Bam a couple of jellybeans.

It is a chilly morning so my gloves and hat are a must. I wrapped my shawl around my neck to keep the chill out.

Dr. Hughes said, "Chelsea you are going to have a great time today. I know it's been a long drive here to Kentucky, but the scenery is worth it. This is one of the most beautiful corners of this state. It is filled with caves and hills and pine trees that look like they are kissing the clouds. It does the heart good to get out and walk with nature."

As we drove deeper and deeper into the woods, snow started falling with flakes as big as golf balls. Never in my life had I seen such a magnificent sight. The dark green pine trees were now dusted with snowflakes and the limbs are heavy in the air. A brown rabbit scurried through the snow with light running steps as if to say, 'follow me', and my eyes did until he was out of sight. As we stopped the car, in front of us are two red birds perched deep inside of an evergreen tree looking like they belonged on the front of a Christmas card.

For the Hughes family, hunting has evolved from a popular recreational activity to a way of life. Dr. Hughes made one of the most profound statements about hunting that I've ever heard, "I compete only with myself when it comes to hunting." He only takes from nature what he needs to feed his family. Every year the family takes this long drive to Kentucky for their Thanksgiving turkey. The main reason is because the birds are plentiful and the state is beautiful. Kentucky was named after the turkey. That is where the last half of the name comes from. He has never failed to bring home a Thanksgiving turkey.

As we walked through the woods we could hear turkeys talking to each other saying, "gobble, gobble, gobble." They were everywhere. The tapestry of their feathers was golden on the tips and a radiant lustrous blue-black at the base. The male bird would spread his tail feathers toward the female bird and dance around as if to say, "Your love is my oxygen, come roost with me." That's just how beautiful his dance was.

Every year, the Hughes family comes to this very spot. They go late in the evening when the birds go to roost. Mrs. Hughes asked me to pick a bird and I pointed at a medium size turkey. She nodded her head to let me know she had her eye on it. She motioned to Dr. Hughes and he nodded. They fired their guns at the exact same moment and two tom turkeys fell to the ground. Zack and I gathered them up and headed for the truck. The feathers are so beautiful that I saved them for a future art project. Zack gave me his bird feathers as well.

I said to Zack, "How can these birds have such beautiful feathers and such an ugly head? By the way, would you remove the birds head and legs? Leave the drumstick though, it's my favorite part of the turkey."

Zack said, "No problem, I sharpened my pocket knife just for these birds. You know, Chelsea, this morning when I talked a little stern to you, the reason was because I thought you were questioning your faith. Once you said to me, 'Can any of you, for all his worries, add one single cubit to his span of life? Mt. 6:27.' When you quoted it, that verse changed my life. I want you to stop worrying and put Jeff in God's hands. Your missing out on the best times of your life over something you have no control over. Leave it in God's hands, pray for Jeff's healing but rejoin the people who miss you. Moping around like you have done for the last four months is not what Jeff would want you to do. From what you told me about him, he would tell you to get back to living."

I gave Zack a hug and he put the birds on ice before we headed back to Oklahoma. Zack's family normally stays the weekend on the turkey shoot because it is such a long drive. They always stay with old friends of the family. This year their friends had something that took them out of state for the weekend, some political fundraiser obligation they could not get out of. Maybe next time we can stay longer and I can tour the caves that Zack talks so much about. What I have seen in this state is breathtaking. I love evergreen trees and this state has the biggest I've ever seen. Glad I made the trip.

The drive home was exhausting and the Hughes family took turns driving, even Zack. At different times we all dozed off, that is except for the driver. When the driver got sleepy it was time to pull over and trade places. It was three in the morning when we finally pulled into my driveway and I was glad to be home. Zack said he would put my bird in their freezer and bring it by in a day or two. That was a relief for me because I was so sleepy and just wanted to go to bed.

It was noon before my eyes opened and my Mom said, "Cloie called and said she left you an email. Did you have a good time with the Hughes family?"

I said, "Yes, Mom we had a great time and Zack will bring our Thanksgiving turkey over in a couple of days. The birds look to weigh around 12 pounds. It was a really long trip, but I enjoyed it. Kentucky is a beautiful state."

I grabbed a bite to eat and checked my emails. Cloie's message was, "Matt asked if he could come to Oklahoma during the Christmas holidays and stay somewhere near our home. Before I answered him I asked Mom if he could stay in my old room and if it is all right with you, can I share your room? Christmas will be here before we know it so I need to let Matt know something soon. Matt told me that Jeff moved his fingers today. The doctor said that is a good sign. Call me."

I first checked to see if Cloie was online because I wanted to talk to her face to face. No luck there, so I called her and told her to get on her computer.

Now we are able to talk face to face and I said, "If you are going to stay in my room we need some ground rules. I play my kind of music and I get up in the mornings when I wake up. If you can live with that you are welcome."

Cloie responded, "Anything you say, little sister, you're the boss of your room. Thank you, I'm so excited about seeing Matt in real life and not just on the computer screen. I'll let him know what a swell little sister I have. Matt talks about you all the time. He gives you full credit for Ed's recovery. Sometimes one gets numb to what family members say to them when they are messing up. An outsider has a fresh approach, and its like a bell goes off in their mind and they see the light. Well, you rang Ed's bell and his family has him back, thanks to you."

"Cloie, thank you for the news of Jeff moving his fingers, that really brightens my day. You know Cloie, when I went to see Jeff in the hospital, just the sight of him with all those tubes stuck in his body made me go completely numb. It was like it wasn't real. The same thing happened yesterday morning when Zack came over. I started thinking Jeff might never wake up and that same numb feeling came over me, I could feel the blood drain from my cheeks, and Zack saw it the moment I opened the door. He was very stern with me and got me to snap back to reality. I now see the importance of thinking positive since Jeff has moved his little finger. Clearly he is on the road to recovery.

Just before Zack had knocked on my door, I was sitting in the corner of the front room all goose-pimply with a great consuming love for Jeff that would ultimately end in human misery because I was thinking he would never wake up. I tried to put myself in Jeff's mind as he lay in a hospital bed for months now and what came into my mind was sadness. He is living in Hell with a self-devouring emptiness that tortures his soul, his vanity and his will to live. Cloie, I just went to a very dark place. Dealing with this for all this time is getting to me. These thoughts are a sobering reminder of how fragile life really is.

I couldn't fathom why Zack was making me squirm with his scrutiny of my belief, or lack of my belief that Jeff would ever wake-up, but now that Jeff has moved his little finger I understand that a more positive attitude is the best thing for Jeff and myself. The news you bring me today has put a new spark of hope in my life.

Enough talk about my dark moods, how is Russia treating you? Mom said you are in a home with a lovely family," I said.

Cloie replied, "Yes, they are a very close knit family who are poor by our standards as far as monetary value, but rich in family values. They are extremely clean and have many family gatherings. Very close knit, and I fit in nicely. I'm very happy. As for you, little sister, I feel your pain as you talk about Jeff, and yes it has been a long time that he has been asleep, but you must know he will wake up. Positive thinking is the only way to deal with this situation, else you waste your life in misery. When Jeff wakes up you will look back and say, "Why did I do that to myself?" I'm with Zack on this one. Stop torturing yourself with this mental anguish. Mental pain makes you weak and vulnerable and I want you strong and proud to be part of Jeff's recovery."

"Big sister, how are things going with you and Matt? There is a lot of distance between you two now that you are in Russia, so how do you deal with it?" I asked.

"Well little sister, I have many more experiences in life than you because I am older. I've learned a lot about love and let me share this with you. When you are in love you are never lonely. You are sharing your life. If you can attain freedom for both partners and love simultaneously without possessiveness, you can live a lifetime together. Freedom must be shared by both people if the relationship is to be true. A jealous heart cannot feel true lasting love, only temporary love that they themselves kill with evil possessiveness. Jealousy is the seed of destruction.

Matt is the most spectacular, intellectual person I've had the pleasure of meeting in my lifetime and he does not hide behind closed doors but lives with the doors wide open. We have yet to be together in the flesh and we only know each other through the computer but there is a connection that neither of us has ever experienced. Satan is spiritually dead, which is why he tempts in the flesh. We have a spiritual connection that is blessed by God. We feed each other's spirit.

For us it was love at first sight. Love at first sight is a powerful force and it has been known to last a lifetime if the high road is always taken. Nobody wants to think of their life as less than a triumph and I think that love is not increased through intimacy unless it is true love and true love is what makes life a triumph for a couple.

If we have in person what we have over the Internet, we will be getting married. Chelsea, you are the first person I have told this to, so please keep it between us. I wanted you to be the first to know because if it weren't for you we would never have met.

Mom always told me, 'You will know true love when you look inside the soul of your lover. You must let their soul become part of you. We relate to each other through the love we share and through our intimacy we are one in a consciousness, we are inside each other's mind. We must provide a consciousness of being loved, happy and fulfilled.' Those were the most powerful words I had ever heard. She told me this when I was 18 years old and it will be with me for my entire life.

With all the distance between Matt and myself we must give each other total freedom and complete trust. The whole of your life consists of physical, emotional, and spiritual experiences that freedom has a direct effect on. The Bible tells it best in 2 Corinthians 3:17, 'Where the Spirit of the Lord is, there is freedom.' God is our Creator; we owe him not to sin. Sin takes away freedom.

In John 4:18 it says, 'There is no fear in love. Perfect love drives out fear, because fear has to do with punishment. The one who fears is not made perfect in love.'

The Bible is the tool Matt and myself use to guide us. Yes, there is a lot of distance between us as far as miles go, but we are one in mind and understand the importance of freedom. With trust comes freedom," Cloie concluded.

"Wow, I knew there was instant chemistry between the two of you, but you are talking marriage without ever even meeting each other in person. I must say I'm surprised, but very happy for you. You will love his family and that is so important in a marriage. I hope Jeff is awake before your wedding day, he so loves his brothers," I said.

"We have no date set. We haven't even had our first kiss, but time is not a factor at this point. I just know Jeff will wake up soon. The doctors say it will happen any time now. His movement is a sure sign that it will happen soon. We won't get married until Jeff is awake. That's how sure we are that Jeff will wake up. It may be six months from now or a year, but we both know he will wake up. Little sister, I have to go now, the family is getting up and I promised to fix breakfast. It should be getting close to time for you to go to bed. I love you, sleep tight and have a wonderful Thanksgiving dinner," Cloie said.

Things sure do move fast in the romance world. I don't know how two people can talk about marriage that have not even held hands or had a kiss. All I can say is we'll see what happens at Christmas when they meet face to face.

Zack brought over my frozen turkey and gave me instructions on when it will thaw and if we don't start cooking it immediately that I should put in the refrigerator until it is time to cook the bird. You would think I knew nothing about cooking with all the instructions he gave me. He means well so I let it go.

Mom put me in charge of cooking the turkey and making the cornbread dressing. This is great because Mrs. Hughes taught me how to make cornbread dressing. I put the turkey in a roasting pan and basted it with butter. Next I stuffed the bird with cornbread mixed with onions, celery, sage, and chicken broth. I sprinkled salt and pepper over the entire dish and popped it in the oven. It is all so simple. I don't know how anybody would think it is an unpleasant task.

Mom made a Waldo salad, which is made with cubed red apples, walnuts, raisins, celery, and plain yogurt. The cranberry sauces spicy aroma filled the air. The potatoes were boiling and the gravy with giblets, hearts, livers and gizzards are looking good. The turkey is placed on a large platter with the dressing all around the edges. A glass of sweet tea is in front of each plate. We joined hands and thanked God for the food we were about to eat. Dad sliced the turkey and served it to each of us. I asked for a whole leg and Mom and Dad had the breast meat. We all agreed that this wild turkey was the best we have ever eaten. That made my day.

Mom emailed Cloie and we all typed a personal note wishing her a Happy Thanksgiving. She will be asleep for several more hours, but when she wakes up, the mail will be there.

I called Jeff's family and they took turns telling me how Jeff has started moving his fingers and I could feel their excitement over the phone. When Ed got on the phone he thanked me for being instrumental in him getting his life back. He talked about how he had become a prisoner to the drugs and how they had stolen his freedom. He talked about how his father and his grandfather had gone to wars for people to have freedom and here he had chosen to be a prisoner by taking his first dose of drugs. He talked about how ashamed he was that he just threw away so many good years of his life, and the damage he caused to his body that will surely shorten his lifespan. Then he thanked me for the words about how his brother Jeff just wanted him back and how my words had made him change his wasteful ways of being an addict.

All the emotions going through my body have somehow made me feel wise beyond my years. I'm experiencing life with all its highs and lows over the last year and that has forced me to grow up in a hurry. I long for the days when life was simple and my biggest decisions were what I would wear to school and what purse should I carry.

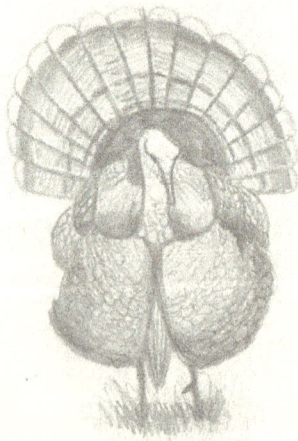

Chapter 8
Christmas

Time is flying and in only a week Cloie will be home for Christmas and we will be sharing my room. I'm so excited because I truly love my big sister. She has always been good to me. The kindness and support she has given me through this whole thing with Jeff has given me the strength to deal with the situation and I thank her for that.

Every morning I jog for an hour to help me stay focused and to keep my spirits up. I learned this from my friend Angela who has occasional struggles with depression. Her doctor demands that she gets plenty of exercise to keep her spirits up. It really has helped and I can tell a difference when I miss a couple of days because of weather.

Bam runs with me and she makes for good company. Sometimes she runs way ahead of me and then she stops and watches me catch up to her. She loves the cold weather and has tons of energy. Her belly is growing large with the new fawn she is carrying. I'm so excited that I have already picked names for a male or a female, whichever it ends up being. The names Prince and Princess will be well suited for the new arrival. When I look at Bam's belly I reminisce over when I first saw Bam as a baby in the arms of my dad's friend. That's how she got her name; my eyes went bam, with excitement. That's a term used by students at my school when something really gets their attention.

My part time job at the mall has made it nice for financial obligations such as gas, insurance and extra spending money, which will be used for Christmas presents.

As I stroll through the mall at a leisurely pace I notice the men's department has a fine looking pair of leather gloves that will be perfect for my dad. Across the aisle are ornaments to decorate a Christmas tree. The first to catch my eye was a porcelain brown cowboy boot with bright red berries and glossy evergreen leaves draped around what would be the ankle part of the boot. The holly against the brown boot is very pleasing to the eye. It is perfect for Jeff's family so I will buy it and get it in the mail today. Next to the boot is a porcelain turkey with brown plumage and a bare red head and neck. Around the feet of the turkey are strands of holly with the bright red berries and glossy green leaves, very similar in color to the boot. This turkey will be perfect for the Hughes family.

As I once again stroll down the aisle of the mall a hand woven hat and scarf catch my eye. This will be perfect for my mom. The set is cream color with a very soft pink border. Mother will look lovely in this combination of colors. For my dad a straw hat. Now it's off to the jewelry department to get a sterling silver ankle bracelet for Cloie. That concludes my Christmas shopping for the day, all for less than $100.

In just two more days Cloie will be home. Excitement is in the air as Dad puts up the tree and I help Mom decorate it. First the twinkling lights, then the bulbs and to top it off an angel goes on the very top branch. Around the bottom is some white fluffy cotton like material, which we lay presents on. When the house lights are out and only the tree lights are on it looks magical and very enchanting.

It's time to go deer hunting and Dad has the truck ready to roll. My mom and I are putting on our boots. There is a light dusting of snow on the ground with a possible chance of a couple of inches more. We only have to travel 50 miles to reach our destination to hunt for a buck deer. If Dad gets lucky and shoots one, we will be serving venison, the meat of a deer, for Christmas dinner.

The air has a biting kind of cold to it and we have been in search of a buck for a couple of hours now. Dad is an excellent tracker and is following a trail left by what he calls a sizeable buck. We have passed by deer because Dad wants a large set of antlers, elongated and branched growths that grow on the heads of male deer, to put over the fireplace in the house.

Suddenly we heard a very large buck call out to a female deer and the sound stopped us in our tracks. He was standing in a clearing unable to see us because of the evergreen trees. We all froze and Dad began to lower his rifle. As he looked through the scope to get a clean shot off the buck turned it's head and looked right at us. Dad fired one shot and the buck melted to the ground without even a quiver. The bullet went right into the heart. Dad immediately tied the bucks back legs with a rope and pulled it onto a tree branch so he could cut the ligaments on the back of the bucks leg. This is important so the meat will taste good. Next he opens up the stomach to get rid of the guts. The truck is about a half mile from where we are and Mom and I went to get it and bring it as close as possible to where the deer is. We have a wagon that holds up to 80 pounds and we are around a block from where Dad is. By the time we got back to the location of where Dad and the buck are, he had him cut up in five large pieces, each weighing around 50 pounds. Dad left the skin on in order to keep the meat clean.

We all helped load the deer meat into the back of

the truck. The head with the large antlers was the last thing to be loaded. It's cold enough that we don't have to worry about the meat going bad. On the way home Dad stopped into the taxidermy office to get the head of the buck stuffed and to have mounting brackets added so he can have it for exhibition above our fireplace. Dad was going to just mount the antlers, but this buck is so beautiful he decided to use the whole head.

Dad finished cutting the buck into large roast and freezing what we call sections for later use. We soaked a hindquarter in a marinade overnight so it would be tender when Mom cooks it.

Cloie will be here tomorrow and I'm so excited. We will both get to meet Matt in person in a couple of days. Jeff has not shown any more signs of waking up. His little finger is the only thing that has moved still. Jeff's mom called today to let me know how much everyone liked the cowboy boot Christmas tree decoration. She said she has baked cookies for my family and Matt was bringing them with him. We talked for around 30 minutes and wished each other's families a Merry Christmas.

Zack came over to pick up a deer roast that my mom promised to give his family. I was completely surprised when I opened the door and there was Zack holding the prettiest pumpkin pie I'd ever seen. He said his mom baked it from scratch. It was still warm from the oven. I invited him in and about that time my mom walked into the room.

Mom said, "Hi Zack, that lovely pie smells heavenly! Come in the kitchen and I'll get your roast ready. Didn't have a chance to tell Chelsea I invited you over. By the way, Chelsea, Zack's family said to tell you thanks for the porcelain turkey for their tree. They loved it."

Zack was big eyed the whole time my mom was talking and was nodding his head in agreement with everything she said. Mom handed Zack his deer roast and we all wished each other Merry Christmas, and he was on his way home.

The sound of the alarm clock came early. We have to be at the airport to pick Cloie up in three hours. We all were scurrying around with light running steps to get dressed, grab a glass of juice and a piece of toast, and head out the door. The roads will be clear of ice and snow so I will do the driving. Last night the tank was filled with gas, the oil and transmission fluids were checked, and the Mustang's windows were washed outside and in.

Dad and Mom brought their cups of coffee with them and they were yawning involuntarily from drowsiness caused by staying up too late last night. Mom wanted all the presents wrapped and placed under the tree so she had more time to spend with Cloie. It must have been midnight before her and Dad got to bed.

The airport was more crowded than I had ever seen it. We had heard earlier on the TV that the weather would be great for air travel and everyone should be able to make it home for the holidays.

Cloie waved at us as she entered the terminal and it was a good thing too because we never would have recognized her with the large fluffy fur hat she was wearing. We all gave each other hugs and kisses on the cheek.

I pointed questioningly at Cloie's large hat and she said, "Oh, its Russian! Do you like it?"

My response, "It nearly swallowed up your head, but I love it. The fur is so shiny."

"I'm glad you like it because everyone is getting one for Christmas!" Cloie said.

We were all exhausted from the drive and Cloie fell asleep in the car. The flight and time change had gotten to her. Cloie's mouth was wide open and she was snoring loud enough to keep me awake at the wheel. I thanked her for that when we got home. Cloie slept for ten straight hours and when she finally woke up we got to hear all about how cold it was in Russia.

Cloie said, "You know how in Oklahoma it only gets below zero occasionally? Well in Russia it stayed below zero most of the winter and seldom got warmer than that. We are talking about bone chilling cold. Everybody wears fur. It's the natural way to stay warm. It's like you spend a lot of energy trying to stay warm, and the only thing that really works is the fur. Nature has it all figured out."

I said, "You're right, Cloie. God didn't give animals synthetic, artificial, chemical compound material that would make them sweat when they started to warm up; he made natural fur for them. Just like he made the animals for human beings so we can wrap ourselves in their fur and leather hide that has been tanned. Animal hides have taken care of human beings since the caveman days. This is nature at it's finest. Natural is how God wants us. Animal hides kept humans alive in the beginning."

Matt called Cloie to see how her flight went and to let her know he would be on his way right after Christmas dinner. He plans to be at our house at 11 p.m. Cloie's face just lights up when she talks about Matt. I completely understand her excitement and can't help but wish Jeff were coming with him. Jeff is always in the back of my mind.

It's Christmas Eve and we have all the Christmas lights on in the backyard. There is a lit up wire deer near the edge of the patio that Bam has become fond of. My favorite decoration is the nativity scene with Baby Jesus, Mary and the three wise men bearing gifts.

It is a family tradition to sit on the backyard patio and sip hot cocoa while we decide what songs we will sing when we go Christmas caroling. We always celebrate Christmas Eve by going from house to house singing Christmas songs of joy and praise. This is our gift to the neighbors. This year we are starting off with Silent Night and ending with Joy to the World.

As we go from house to house we pick up some of the young people who want to join in on spreading the joy of singing. By the time we were finished we had a total of fifteen carolers. We walked each back to their homes and called it a night.

I woke in the morning to the smell of sausage frying. As I stumble into the kitchen, Dad greets me with, "Good morning sunshine." I wave to say hi, while rubbing the sleep from my eyes. I'm slow to wake up in the morning and everyone accepts this about me. I sat down at the table and Dad poured a glass of juice and sat it in front of me. Juice always helps me get started. As I finished my glass of juice, Cloie gave Dad a hug and sat down beside me. I poured her a glass of juice and Mom walked in the kitchen from the living room.

She had been up for a while and hugged Cloie's neck in one arm, and my neck in the other and said, "Merry Christmas, my beautiful daughters." We each gave her a kiss on the cheek and wished her the same.

Dad said, "Biscuits and gravy for everyone. There's nothing like sausage gravy with lots of black pepper."

After everyone finished breakfast we opened presents. Everyone was pleased with his or her gifts. Mom said for Cloie and I to go have fun and that she would clean up and put the deer roast on to cook.

Cloie asked if I wanted to help get Matt's room ready, seeing how he will be here tonight sleeping in her bed. She is so excited that as she stripped the sheets from her bed she began singing. She made up a little tune when she was very young and very happy. To this day when she gets super excited she sings this little tune and it goes like this. "I'm as light as a feather blowing in the wind, not a care in the world, just living a dream. My mind takes me places that I've never seen, no sadness or grief, what a relief. A dream it may be, so good it does seem."

Cloie said, "Chelsea, do you think Matt would like the hunter green sheets or the beige and brown striped set?"

I laughed, "The green sheets look like a Christmas package."

"Yes, aren't you the funny one today. In a way he is a gift from God. I believe God has sent Matt to me because I have waited for the right man to be part of my life. If more people could just hold out until the perfect match came their way, there would not be so many broken homes or babies being born out of wedlock. You see, Chelsea, family is the most important thing in life and if it takes waiting until you are in your twenties to find your soul mate, then so be it. I think everyone has someone who is right for them; the problem with most people is that they are in too big of a hurry to start life. Our mom has given us the guidance necessary to save ourselves for our wedding day. My wedding day will be special in every way, including my first time to make love. Our mom gave me permission to deny the media and society and delay sex. We are so lucky, Chelsea, to have a mom to guide us on the road of life," Cloie said.

I just love it when Cloie gets up on her soapbox and starts talking about how to protect your destination. She reinforces what my mom preaches to me about all the time. Mom takes it a step further talking about the risks of contracting an STD. Mom says that people who have many sexual partners are being careless because of all the sexually transmitted diseases that are out there. Mom says it is as if a person has sex with everyone else their current sexual partner has ever encountered before sexually.

My mom told me if I decided to have sex that she would take me to the doctor to get a vaccination shot for STDs. Mom told me vaccinations for STDs should always be considered for the protection of our body. There is still a high risk present despite the proper use and availability of the latest condom. Mom says that condoms are only a risk reduction, not a complete protection from a STD or a broken heart. Also, contracting an STD in most cases is a lifelong sentence. AIDS is on the rise and will end your life early. It's a lot to think about.

We got Matt's room put together and the excitement of his arrival was mounting. Cloie is so sure that they are perfect for each other that she is talking about what their children will look like. I hope he is thinking the same thing because they would make the perfect couple. Cloie is smart and sassy and has saved herself for marriage. That's right, she held out for a better more meaningful life. She has avoided the emotional scars that sexual encounters leave behind. If Matt and Cloie get married, what a wedding present she will be giving Matt.

After we got Matt's room ready for him we went outside to shoot a few hoops. I suggested it hoping to get some of the excess energy out of Cloie. She is about to burst with excitement. It is understandable seeing how they will be with each other in person for the first time instead of over the Internet. There is an enormous difference because they will finally be able to touch each other, even being able to smell each other, which is not possible over the Internet.

We bundled up, me in my new sports jacket with a hoodie and Cloie in her new scarf and matching hat and gloves. We weren't out for blood in this match, just a little exercise. Cloie had not lost her skills with the basketball and was shooting amazingly well. She was on a high and it was showing in her ability to shoot hoops. She made five in a row before she was even warmed up, but maybe the thought of Matt being here tonight had her warmed up.

Dad and Mom were watching us through the window and Cloie waved them over to join us.

Mom opened the door and said, "We will be right there, the roast is on and I have some time for play. We just need to bundle up." It is a cold but sunny day, and the air is still. A perfect winter's day. The exercise did all of us some good. An hour of vigorous and energetic basketball was perfect for holding us over until Christmas supper was done.

Mom and Dad talked about how excited they were about meeting Matt tonight. In almost the same breath they told me how they said their prayers for Jeff's recovery. Cloie gave me a hug and said that she also said prayers this morning for Jeff and his family, as she does every morning. It was a very warm hug and I needed it.

I whipped up a pineapple upside down cake and slipped it into the oven right after Mom pulled out the deer roast. The cake only needed thirty minutes to cook and the roast always sits for that long before Dad slices it. Cloie set the table while Mom made a salad. Dad put ice in the glasses and poured the tea. We all had a hand in putting Christmas dinner on the table. When I pulled my cake from the oven it was time to sit down for dinner, join hands and thank God for this bounty we are about to eat.

Dad said grace and he began with, "Our health is the most precious gift life has. We protect it with these God given live plants that will nourish our cells. We thank you God for this wild clean meat that you helped me find to provide for this Christmas meal. Our bodies are your temples and we cherish them with all that is good. We thank you God for bringing our family together to celebrate this Christmas feast."

Dad always speaks from his heart when he prays over our meals. We never know what will come out of his mouth, but it is always good.

Cloie asked nonchalantly with her eloquent voice, "Chelsea, would you please pass me the salad?" With that we began to eat Christmas dinner. The deer meat was tender enough to cut through with a fork and the yams were as sweet as honey. The pineapple upside down cake was yummy and we have leftovers enough to eat this all again tomorrow.

The excitement of Matt staying with us for a few days was mounting. There is a good energy in the whole house. I refuse to dwell on the fact that Jeff can't come with Matt or to dwell on his current condition. I'm going to enjoy Matt's company and be happy for my sister.

I read a passage in the Bible this morning, Mark 8:22-25, and it said, "When they arrived at Bethsaida, some people brought him a blind man and begged him to touch him. Jesus took the blind man's hand and led him outside the village. Putting spittle on his eyes he laid his hands on him and asked, "Can you see anything?" The man opened his eyes and said, "I can see people but they look like walking trees!" Then a second time Jesus laid hands on his eyes, and he saw perfectly; his sight was restored and he could see everything clearly."

If Jesus had to pray twice, then I will continue to pray for Jeff and except whatever God's plan is for him.

Cloie has disappeared to her room and was putting the finishing touches on what she thinks Matt will need such as fresh towels, washcloths, an unopened bar of soap and toothpaste. After Matt's room was finished, Cloie began getting herself ready for when Matt walks in the door. When she finished and walked into the living room, we all dropped our jaws at the sight of her. Mom said, "You look great, honey!"

"Thanks Mom, I feel amazing in my new outfit with my hair put on top of my head looking like royalty. Do you think Matt will like the way I look?" Cloie asked.

"If not, he can turn around and go home. I'm so glad that I get to share this good feeling with you. I can feel your excitement," said Dad.

I said, "I have the ultimate compliment for you big sister. Matt will see that your mind is as beautiful as your body, and that's what really counts."

"Leave it to you little sister who is wise beyond your

years," Cloie said.

Matt's car engine got our attention and Cloie said, "He's thirty minutes early! Oh my gosh, I'm so excited!"

Dad said, "I will go out and escort him into the house, everyone just calm down."

Our front window has a tint that allows you to look out, but people cannot see in. Dad met Matt on the front porch and they began discussing the traffic and how easy our place was to find with Matt's GPS locator when Cloie blurted out, "He is a machine of perfection. Truly the man of my dreams." Mom and I looked at one another all wide eyed and once again silence filled the room as we gazed upon Matt. There is a tension in the silence as we wait for when he will stop talking to Dad and get in this house. Pardon my impatience, but I thought he was here to see Cloie, and not to spend all night showing Dad his supremely confident personality.

Ten minutes has passed and they are still on the front porch talking. Cloie is starting to get edgy, filled with nervous tension. Finally she couldn't take it anymore. "I'm going out there," she said. As she reached to open the door, Matt opened it at the same moment. As soon as he saw her, his face lit up and he took her in his arms and gave her a kiss on the forehead.

He then said quietly, "You look lovely," and as he stepped back he looked at her from her head to her toes and then back up to her eyes, all the while holding her hands. It was so sweet the way he portrayed his raw charisma during their first physical contact. Cloie dropped one of Matt's hands and they turned around to face us. My heart was pounding with excitement.

As they stepped into the living room Cloie grabbed my hand and said, "Matt I would like you to meet my sister Chelsea in person once again."

Matt shook my hand and then gave me a hug and

said, "I want to thank you for bringing Cloie into my life," and then turned to Mom and hugged her and said, "Thank you for raising your daughter to have the morals that make her as beautiful inside as she is on the outside."

Mom smiled at Matt and said, "You are as eloquent as you are kind."

Matt has a way with words, a combination of artistry and charm that steals our hearts. Matt went to his car to get the cookies his mother had baked for our family. Then he went back to get his overnight bag in one hand and a sapling tree in the other.

Matt handed Mom the cookies and said, "From my family to yours," and then he turned to me and handed me the sapling and said, "Jeff planted a pear tree some years ago and the sapling came up from one of the seeds of that tree's fruit. I wanted you to have this sapling and I will plant it for you tomorrow. Jeff is crazy about you, Chelsea, and I know he would be pleased that you have this tree as a reminder of how he feels about you."

A tear rolled down my cheek and dripped into the pot of the sapling that I was now holding. I sniffled a laugh and said, "This little fellow needed a drink." I wiped my cheek and looked up at Matt and said, "I would love for you to help me break up the frozen ground. I know just where we can plant it. We just looked at each other in silence."

Mom broke the silence saying, "Well, these cookies you brought look delicious! Milk anyone?" We all raised our hands and before we took our first bite Mom said, "Thank you Lord for bringing Matt to our house safely and for these cookies we are about to eat, Amen."

Cloie took the first bite and said, "These are scrumptious, be sure to tell your mom we think she is great at cooking cookies!" It was getting late so Mom and Dad headed to bed first, and a little later I turned in. Cloie and Matt needed some alone time.

When morning came I slipped out of my room quietly so as not to wake Cloie. I don't know what time she finally came to bed because I was asleep. She was in a full snore with her mouth wide open again, so it didn't look like she would be getting up any time soon. The sapling was left on the front porch and I quietly stepped out the door to be sure it was still there, and then I touched it softly. Jeff is part of this little twig. It is possible he ate the very pear that the sapling came from. One of Jeff's favorite things was to pick a ripe pear from the tree and eat it on the spot. Jeff would say that he wanted to eat it while it was still alive because that is when it is the best, fresh off the tree. I spoke to Jeff's spirit and said that I would cherish the fruit from this tree as he had. When I speak of Jeff's spirit it is his soul, the divine invisible part of his body that I am talking about. The spirit never dies like the flesh does, which is why we must protect our essence of the soul, as if refining it, extracting impurities. Our karma must win the struggle between good and evil, for eternity never ends. Whatever happens with Jeff, if this is only a near death experience or he dies, his good spirit lives on for eternity. That is the life after death that God has promised us. I will always speak to Jeff's spirit.

Mom came out the door with a cup of hot cocoa for me. She handed it to me and said, "I remember when we were in Florida and you first met Jeff. You told me how he told the story about planting a pear tree so his body could have the needed potassium found in pears to feed his muscles. I couldn't think of a nicer present for you. Matt thinks deep thoughts and I like that about him. Cloie and Matt make a perfect couple."

Matt helped me plant the pear tree and after that he and Cloie went off to do some sightseeing. They were gone the whole day only to return for supper. When everyone finished eating and the dishes were washed Cloie and Matt asked if they could talk to us as a family.

Matt was holding Cloie's hand and said, "Mr. and Mrs. Songbird, I would like to ask your permission to marry your daughter this May after I graduate from college. I promise to treat her with respect and love. We are vibrating in concert and therefore are experiencing a heightened sense of love and if we can have your blessing we plan to marry in May and return to Russia so Cloie can finish her degree in foreign language. After she graduates from college we will make the decision of where to live and raise a family. If you need time to discuss this I understand and will wait patiently."

Dad took control of this conversation by saying, "Cloie, is this something you want out of life?"

"Yes, Dad, I'm so in love with Matt and can hardly wait to commit my entire lifetime to him. Please give us your blessing, it will mean so much to us," Cloie said.

"No need to beg," said Dad smiling, "The two of you were made for each other, just like your mom and I were. You have my blessing. You have made a good choice. Matt is a real man, mentally and physically. The two of you will make a great family," Dad said.

"Thank you for your daughter's hand in marriage, you will be proud of the way we raise our future family," Matt said.

I knew this was going to happen in my heart, but I hadn't realized it was going to happen with such class. It was a great experience to watch Matt ask for Cloie's hand in marriage. I've known they are perfect for each other for some time and it felt good to hear them talk about it. Cloie has not been very lucky at love in the past, but she had enough sense to know that eventually the right man would come along and not to worry about it. The two of them are simply a perfect match.

Cloie was beaming the whole time Matt stayed with us. I have now seen the face of mature love and realize if you wait long enough and you are willing to be unselfish in a relationship, you will find the person who is meant for you.

Chapter 9
The Awakening

It was great to have Cloie home for the holidays and to finally meet Matt in person. He asking her to marry him was so exciting. When people are in love as these two are, the air fills with their excitement. Mom and Dad are glowing at the thought of becoming grandparents in a couple of years and if Cloie and Matt have children that means I will become an aunt. The whole thing is just heart warming.

Everyday that I come home from school or from my part time job at the mall, the first thing I notice is the sapling pear tree that Matt brought and helped me plant. When I see it, thoughts of Jeff pop into my mind. He has yet to open his eyes but he moves his whole body now, like he is stretching, which is what you do right before you wake up. Jeff's mom has been very good to me through this whole thing by staying in contact and letting me talk to Jeff while she holds the phone to his ear. It makes me feel close to him and also as if I'm helping him to wake up. The brain is an amazing organ that can respond to stimulation like no other part of the body. Actually it does control every muscle and every feeling in the body. It makes me feel good inside when I talk to Jeff on the phone, even if it is only a one way conversation, to know that I have a small part in his recovery, and it is enough to keep me going.

Ed is still going to rehab but is off drugs. He has started going to college and his major is accounting. He says that numbers never lie; if you work the problem correctly the outcome will always be the same. Ed says he has had enough lies to last a lifetime. Ed says he is in search of his soul mate to end his lonely heart blues. Part of Ed's reason for beginning drug use was behind a broken heart. His yearlong girlfriend dumped him and he began consuming alcohol. Next came the drugs that helped him forget being dumped, but the worst part of that was that it made him forget everybody who still loved him. This is why drugs are the big lie. They hurt you, not help you.

Ed fell in love with the way someone looked, not with what they were inside. He wants his eyes to no longer rule his heart, so he is in search of an ugly woman with a good personality to see if she can change his way of looking at people. He needs to start dating and find the right woman. Ed will always seek counseling to help him stay on track. He knows he is vulnerable to temptation of being persuading to use the quick fix of drugs that could ruin his life once again. He's just not strong enough to deal with rejection, so he has decided not to put himself in that position again. He will let the girl tell him she is in love with him first instead of putting his heart out to be broken. This is his choice and his way of protecting himself.

Cloie emailed me today to share her excitement of having her dress tailor made for her wedding. She has chosen white silk with streams of white lace. The veil will be as long as the dress in the back and a small piece of lace in the front to cover her face. Matt will remove it from her face right before he seals their wedding day with a kiss. Cloie requested that Mom pick out the flowers and put me in charge of the dresses for the bridesmaids. She also asked me to be her maid of honor. Cloie chose the color turquoise for my dress and a lighter bluish green for the three bridesmaids dresses. Dad is put in charge of the tuxedos for the guys. Instead of the standard black tie, their ties will match the dresses of whom they escort down the aisle. Matt will be the only one wearing a black tie.

Most weddings are planned six months in advance, we only have five months and the bride is in Russia. This is truly going to be a challenge.

I emailed Cloie back and said that I would be thrilled to be her maid of honor and that I would be proud to wear my favorite color, turquoise. Mom added to the email that she also is honored to pick the flowers and asked if she should also order the brides cake and the groom's cake.

As I continued to check my emails, my computer said, "You have mail." When I answered the mail it was Jeff's mail. It was Jeff's mom requesting that I video chat with her right then, because Jeff had opend his eyes earlier that day!

I turned on the web cam and when she appeared she said, "Our prayers have been answered! Chelsea, I want to thank you for your dedication to my son. You have been responsible for Ed getting treatment for his drug problem and now your prayers have been answered for Jeff. My son Matt will soon be marrying Cloie and that will officially make us family. I thank God for you every day."

"I am so excited! Tell me everything he said! Is he walking? What did he have for breakfast?" I said, barely able to contain myself.

Jeff's mom replied, "Hold your horses, we must take it slowly, one step at a time. First of all, he has just now opened his eyes. The doctor said that because he was unconscious for so long recovery is going to take a while. Jeff is still being fed through a tube and he has not spoken or walked yet. The doctor says that because he has been without conscious thought or feeling or even psychologically aware of his surroundings, he may not remember many things. An example the doctor gave was that he would have to be taught how to tie his shoelaces again. Right now I'm just happy to look into his big beautiful eyes."

My heart has a song in it that is full of undeniable joy. It is as if a 200-pound weight has been lifted off my shoulders. I ran through the house, singing, Jeff is awake! Jeff is awake! My mom joined me step for step and Dad looked up at us like we'd lost our minds.

Finally he said, "Will you two settle down and tell me what is going on?" Mom hugged me and said that she was so happy for me. Mom can relate to me almost as if she can read my mind. Dad on the other hand always needs things explained to him. I began with, "Jeff's mom had a little visit with me on the web cam and Jeff has opened his eyes! It will be a slow process getting him back to his old self, but with time he should function like his old self again. I'm so excited! Hopefully he can be his brother's best man at the wedding. It would be a dream come true to have Jeff escort me down the aisle on my sister's wedding day."

Dad said, "Chelsea, that is such great news! Be careful about making plans too soon though."

"I can't help it, I can see it in my mind as if it is happening right this very moment," I said.

My dad is such a realist that things have to actually be happening before he can get excited. Never mind him, right now I am living the excitement of Jeff's awakening. I'm out the front door to hug the sapling that came from the seed of the tree that Jeff planted to nourish his body. He is in the process of recovery and today, that's all that matters to me.

The process is truly too slow for Jeff's recovery. He is at home now with his family, but his memory is a far cry from where it needs to be. He can walk and eat and even bathe himself, but he can't tie his shoelaces. His mother is having a great time teaching him. It is so amazing how one's appreciation is heightened for a love one when you almost lost them to an accident. They consume your thoughts and cares. They are always on your mind.

Cloie emailed me to see how the dresses are coming along. I contracted the dress making to a local tailor not far from our home. My dress is finished so I modeled it for Cloie over the web cam. She told me how proud she is of me for being responsible enough to help with the wedding. She also told me that I had impeccable taste in the design of my dress. I let her know that the tailor was working on the other two dresses and they will be just as beautiful.

The wedding will be in a month and everything is falling into place. Cloie wants an outdoor wedding in our backyard. Dad has ordered the rental of an oversize white tent in case it rains. He has put in his order for 100 white fold up chairs. Better to have too many than not enough.

Jeff's mom calls or emails me daily and allows Jeff to hear my voice or see my face but he has no recollection of who I am. Whatever God has planned for us I'm willing to accept. I'm just so glad that Jeff is awake. That is enough. We will be walking down the aisle as the best man and maid of honor at my sister's wedding, and right now that is enough for me.

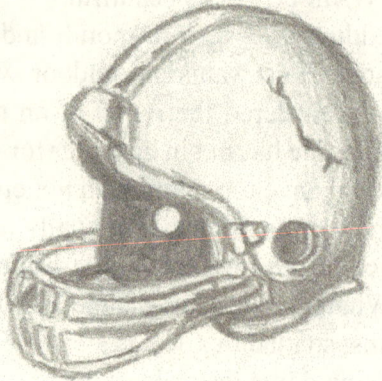

Chapter 10
The Wedding

Cloie is home on spring break from Russia and she has that beaming look that brides-to-be have right before their wedding. In just one week she will be Mrs. Cloie Hall.

The wedding dress that Cloie had made in Russia is amazing. It is the whitest silk and lace I've ever seen. It's as if it has a glow. She will be a lovely bride.

We have a trail in the wildlife refuge that we run on barefooted, weather permitting, for a mile. It is great exercise for the body to run barefooted, for it lines up the bones in the body the way nature meant for them to be. We always feel better after a barefoot run, especially today.

Mom and Dad went into the house and Cloie and I sat outside and began a heart to heart talk.

Cloie said, "You know little sister, the game of love begins where girls pretend to be attractive to get love while boys pretend to be taken away with you to get sex. It's all a crazy game until you find the right person to spend the rest of your life with. An emotional price is paid with every break up so the fewer boyfriends you have the better off you are. If you are patient, the right man will come your way, this I have learned. Years ago, I said to myself after a breakup,

'Will I let my misguided humility lead me to ruin or will I work harder to get a few things modestly right in my lifetime on earth?' This is when I took a break from dating, and Matt came into my life because of you introducing us over the Internet. I never would have dreamed my future husband would come to me through technology and my little sister. Life can be strange. Let me put reality in a nutshell: love will find you when you least expect it. Love is a process and is seldom a permanent condition; this is proven by the divorce rate. Desire can saturate the imagination and people let their desires take control of their lives. Love must go deeper than just desire; it must reach a level of unselfish, generous attitude toward each other. Matt taught me this. I truly believe this time I have gotten it right. I'm so glad I waited for the right man to be part of my forever. Now little sister, I want to know what is going on in your mind."

"Well, to start, I'm excited that Jeff is going to be walking me down the aisle in your wedding, even if he hasn't a clue as to who I am. I most certainly will enjoy his company. I do hope that when I feel his hand I get that wonderful feeling again though, and it will jolt his memory. There is something spontaneous about the touch of his hand on mine that altered my rate of breathing. Enough of that, I've put it into God's hands and I am willing to accept whatever his plan is for us. This time is for you, Cloie, I don't want to cloud it up with my stuff," I said.

The tent and chairs have arrived and the rental company is setting things up. It's two days before the wedding and we want everything in place so we will have time to entertain Matt's family. We want all the stress to be gone so we can have a fantastic time. Mom and Cloie went to town when Dad received a phone call from Matt's father saying they had made it to the hotel. Dad told them to rest up and that Cloie was taking care of some last minute details. He said she should be home soon and he would have her call as soon as she got home. He went on to ask how their trip went and other chitchat, which always makes people feel welcome.

Excitement is in the air. When Cloie and Mom walked through the door I just burst out saying, "They're here, they're here!" Mom tried to settle me down and Cloie was immediately on the cell phone calling Matt.

Mom said, "They are early; this is good. We will have a chance to get to know each other before rehearsal. I'm starting to get excited."

The people who set up the tent have finished placing the chairs and the long rug that covers the grass leading to the wildlife refuge. The rug's purpose is to keep the bride's dress from getting dirty. Cloie has a long trail that is about eight feet that drags behind her. Dad will help her carry it until she is on the rug, then they will let it drag behind her with all its beauty.

Cloie was off the phone and said, "They are ready to come over and I want Chelsea to come with me to their hotel so they can follow us to the house. I would hate for them to get lost. Besides that, I have not met them in person like Chelsea has. I need to meet Matt's parents before I introduce them to my parents, don't you think?"

Mom said, "Absolutely, Cloie. Besides, I need to check on how the flowers are coming around. You two take your time."

"Hey Cloie, I'll drive," I said.

We loaded up and were on our way. It is a beautiful spring day and the foliage is thicker than I ever remember it being. The wind is as quiet as a mouse. The stillness will certainly add to the enchantment of the wedding. Hopefully it will continue for the wedding tomorrow.

As we pulled up to the hotel, Matt was outside ready to greet us. Cloie jumped out of the car and was in Matt's arms before I even turned it off. It is a heart-warming sight.

As I walked towards Matt, I extended my hand to him but he grabbed me around the waist and pulled me into a group hug with my sister. I feel so welcomed. Matt gave me a forewarning that Jeff will be different than I remember him and that it will take a lot of time before he is back to his old self again. I nodded in acknowledgement and we went inside for Cloie to meet Matt's parents in person.

When the door opened my eyes went straight to Jeff. It was as if all sound disappeared. Jeff seemed to be in a daze and did not even acknowledge my presence. He does not know who I am, I realized.

Mr. and Mrs. Hall had finished meeting Cloie, which had just seemed like background noise to me until Matt said, "This little girl named Chelsea Songbird is responsible for the event of the year, Matt and Cloie becoming the new Mr. and Mrs. Hall. Let's all give her a big hand." Everyone clapped, including Jeff. The difference was that he had a blank look on his face, like he wasn't really sure what was going on.

Mrs. Hall took Jeff by the hand and nodded at me with her head to follow them out the door. When the door closed behind us, she introduced me to Jeff and we shook hands. The feeling we had once shared at the touch of our hands had disappeared. I know it showed on my face because Mrs. Hall immediately tried to explain to Jeff how we had met before and exactly who I was. He just shrugged his shoulders, like he remembered nothing of what she said.

She then turned to me and said, "The doctor told us it will take a lot of time before Jeff totally recuperates his memory. We must take it slowly. Do you understand, Chelsea?"

"Yes, I understand. I promise, you won't have a problem with me because Jeff means the world to me whether he remembers me or not and I want nothing but the best for him," I said.

With that, we went back inside and joined the others. Matt was in the middle of a story about how his family and friends looked like a convoy going down the highway. It took ten rooms at the hotel to house them all. That reminded me, "Where is Ed?"

"He went across the street for some apple juice," answered Matt with a smile, "That is his new addiction. Anyways, that's what he calls it. We all accept that kind of language from him because it keeps him aware of his problem and that's a good thing. When an addict starts denying that they have a problem is when you need to start worrying."

Just then, Ed walked through the door with his apple juice and a big smile on his face.

"I thought that might be you two when I saw that hot little turquoise mustang sitting out front," he said.

He extended his hand to Cloie and while they were shaking hands he said, "Congratulations on taking my brother off our hands, I wish you both the best."

Ed then turned to me and said with his hand extended for a shake, "Chelsea, thank you for giving me back my life. You are my hero."

Before we knew it we were back at our house and everyone was getting to know one another. Rehearsal will start in about an hour and the dinner will be at a fine restaurant chosen by my father. He's paying for it so we all agreed on his choice.

The morning of my big sister's wedding was truly a joyous time for the family. Cloie is still in bed and it is two hours before she has to be at the beauty shop. Mom said to let her sleep because it was her day and she is certain that there is nothing but sweet dreams going on in her head. Mom handed me a cup of tea and a piece of toast with apple butter she had canned last year. It hit the spot. I joined Dad in the backyard under the tent.

He said, "You know, Chelsea, I rented this tent

because it might rain, but I am glad I did anyway because it provides great shade. I am a happy man today because your sister is making the right choice in marrying Matt. He is the right person for her. I used to worry for her because she was not picking the right people to date. Well, maybe it was the other way around. The wrong people were picking her. Anyway, Cloie picked Matt and he is a perfect match for her. His family fits well with ours, which is another plus."

The chairs are filling up with guests and Cloie is putting on her veil. The time for the event of the year is upon us. Cloie is going through everything to do, something borrowed, which is the necklace she made for me that says 'I love you' in Cherokee made from white and turquoise beads. Something used, which is a handkerchief of Dad's in case she cries. For something new, Mom bought her real turquoise earrings. Cloie is ready to walk down the aisle, so I give her a kiss on the cheek, tell her what a lovely bride she is, and I leave to walk down the aisle with Jeff as maid of honor and him as the best man. The guests could not see us because of the wooden fence, and we met near the pond to begin the wedding procession. We all look stunning in our dresses and our tuxedos.

The air is filled with the sweet smells of honeysuckle and pink roses. The music suddenly begins and Jeff hooks his arm in mine and the wedding begins. As I walk down the aisle, Jeff seems foreign to me. Like a stranger I have never met. It is very difficult to understand how a person can lose the feelings of a touch they once had. I guess those feelings were coming from the brain and it must be a two-way connection. Otherwise I would still feel it on my end, but I don't feel anything but the flesh of his hand. The electric feelings we had before the accident are not here.

The wedding song has begun and I see just a glimpse of Cloie's white dress through the thick lush green foliage. As the music plays Cloie and Dad appear. The guests are on their feet and are looking in anticipation for their first glimpse of the bride. As Cloie steps on to the carpet and Dad releases the trail of her dress and veil, they drag behind Cloie in all their splendor.

I can feel the joy in that air; it is electric. Cloie and Dad look marvelous as they walk down the aisle, arms locked in support of one another. The guests look on in astonishment and wonder at the beauty this bride brings to this blessed day. Cloie stops for a moment to hug Mom and give her a kiss on the cheek, then she turns to Mrs. Hall and hugs her tightly. Dad gets Cloie to the altar and gives her to Matt, then turns and joins Mom as one of the guests. Cloie and Matt turn to watch the ring bearers, Matt's niece and nephew, both age six, walk down the aisle with their wedding rings on a pillow. They take the rings and the vows begin. They slip the rings on one another's fingers and seal their marriage with a kiss.

The words, "I now pronounce you man and wife," are said and just like that, they became Mr. and Mrs. Hall.

After the preacher introduced Matt and Cloie as man and wife, everyone in the wedding procession lined up while the guests filed through and shook our hands and introduced themselves. The guests loved the outside wedding and some of them told me they were looking forward to my wedding so they can do this again.

Cloie and Matt were stuffing cake in each other's mouth when Ed stepped up beside me.

He said, "I'm so proud of the choice my brother has made for a wife. They were tailor made for each other. I was looking around at all her friends, but they are much too pretty for me. I'm into ugly but interesting."

I could not help but chuckle at Ed's seriousness in his quest for an ugly mate and he responded to my laugh with, "There is nothing funny about what I said. I'm dead serious. Good looking people that are actually good people are hard to find. I'm searching for a woman and her looks don't matter to me. Let me give you an example. If you have a beautiful piece of artwork on your wall, at first you are all taken with it, but after a while it just becomes part of the wall. Most of the time you don't even notice it unless someone calls it to your attention. This is why I think that once I get used to an ugly woman that I am in search of, it won't matter what she looks like. I just want her to make me a good wife."

"Not to change the subject, but don't you think we should go get some cake and punch before its all gone?" I said.

"Sure, let's get in line. Let me explain why I need an ugly woman. You see, Chelsea, I'm very selfish and possessive. An ugly woman isn't accustomed to having someone be possessive of her, so she would love the attention, while a pretty woman probably wouldn't. An ugly woman wouldn't be able to get enough of me. Our personalities would be a great match."

We got our cake just in time for the wedding dance. The organ player introduced two guitar players who were helping him out with the music. Then the music started and Cloie and Matt were in each other's arms. They were graceful with their expressive dips and long strides and were in perfect sync with the music. They were so fluent in their moves they looked like one entity.

Ed said, "They are a work of art."

After their dance it was time for Cloie to throw her bouquet of pink roses into a cluster of single females. She threw it high and BreAnna jumped up and grabbed it like it was a basketball. Everyone clapped for her athletic ability. I even heard one woman say, "She can have that bouquet of roses, she is too physically strong for me to go up against." That put a smile on my face. I made my way through the crowd of people and hugged BreAnna's neck.

I said, "I was wondering if you came; I didn't even see you until now."

BreAnna answered, "I was sitting in the back. I wouldn't have missed this for the world!"

"You know, you are actually the only friend of mine that knows Cloie. Come with me, I want to introduce you to Jeff. He is not allowed to have a lot of excitement; his mother is very protective of him right now. Take it slow and keep it calm, okay?" I said.

Jeff and his mom were over to the side of the crowd by themselves. I introduced BreAnna as my best friend, but there was not much reaction out of Jeff. He just nodded his head and look away. Mrs. Hall on the other hand talked a blue streak. She was impressed with BreAnna's ability to jump. After all, she had three boys who were very athletic and she took notice when she saw someone with such ability.

I went in search of my mom and dad so BreAnna could say hello. When I saw them they were talking to the newly married couple, the perfect time to introduce my friend to Matt.

"This way, BreAnna, we have them all together here," I said.

Mom noticed us heading their way and said, "Hey girls! Matt, this is Chelsea's friend BreAnna."

Matt said, "Yes, you are the one who caught the roses. If we had any scouts here looking for soccer goalies, they would be fighting over you right now. That was amazing!"

Some of the young people were tying strings of cans to Cloie's jeep and writing 'Just married' all over the windows. They were passing out little bundles of birdseed to throw at the newlyweds when they left. The old tradition of throwing rice has been found to hurt birds. They lack the ability to digest the rice unless it is cooked. I don't think the bride and groom would want boiled rice in their hair.

No one except Mom and Dad know where the honeymooners are off to, and they aren't telling. This is their weeklong wedding present, picked out by Mom. Hope they enjoy themselves.

Chapter 11
Soccer

School will be out soon for the summer and my diving lessons are going well. I can stay under water for quite some time now without panicking.

BreAnna took what Matt said about scouts fighting over her seriously. She has been studying up on the game of soccer in the library and she thinks she actually would make an excellent goalkeeper. During our lunch hour BreAnna shared some of her thoughts with Angela, Sara and myself about joining a summer club soccer team for girls.

BreAnna said, "All you need are shin guards, cleats, and a soccer ball. How about we all go to a field today and try out the new soccer ball I bought? Let's just kick it around a little and see if it might be something we all could have fun with this summer."

After school we met at a soccer field and BreAnna laid out a game plan for us. Right now, she is the only one who knows anything about the game, so we are all ears.

"Goalkeeping is what the group must have in

order to become a winning team. The goalkeeper can launch attacks and save goals. We are here today to see if I am any good at that position or if any of you three are good at it. I'm going to guard this net and you are going to try to kick the ball past me into the area covered by the net. We will keep it simple for today," she said.

This is actually a lot of fun. BreAnna is doing a fair job at keeping the ball out of the goal. Angela is also a pretty good goalkeeper. Sara and I are not as good because we are shorter and have a hard time getting the high balls, but we are pretty good at scoring goals.

We took a break and BreAnna seems to think we all have potential to develop into being a good soccer team.

"Angela, I want to tell you a little bit about goalkeeping. You seem to be very good at it, so I want to share with you some of my knowledge about the position. Goalkeepers are the only players allowed to control the ball with their hands. They wear gloves but I only had enough money for a ball, so next week I plan to buy the gloves. I will pick up a pair for you as well. You can use your hands within the penalty area, which is 44 yards wide and 18 yards out from the end line of the field. You have the height to catch the ball with your hands, which is definitely a plus in soccer. The goal is 8 feet high and 24 feet wide. You are able to jump high enough to stop any of these balls that are hit with a player's head or kicked high. Yes, head butting the ball is legal in soccer. A player can leave the ground early, before the ball's arrival, and then strike it with the flat surface of their forehead. You must remember to tuck your chin, keep your eyes open and your mouth closed."

BreAnna is serious about the game of soccer. Neither of us played basketball this year due to our jobs and we really missed playing sports. I am excited about being with my friends this summer and I love sports of any kind. Learning to play the game of soccer will be a perfect activity for the summer.

I went to the library and checked out a book about soccer to learn for myself about the game. BreAnna is focused on goalkeeper and that seems to be all she is talking about. I need to learn about the sport so whatever position fits my ability I will begin focusing on.

I had no idea that billions of people around the world watch soccer games on television. The soccer game most watched is the FIFA world cup. I'm having a hard time wrapping my mind around the fact that billions of people could be watching the same game at the same time. That's just a lot of people for a game I never gave much thought, until BreAnna took an interest in it.

The game was named soccer 150 years ago in England and the United States also calls it soccer, however most people around the world call it football.

The game is very physical and you can hit a flying ball with your head. I think practicing kicking the ball and trapping the ball with my foot will be how I start out learning about soccer. The position forward, who is the person who tries to score the goals, is perfect for me. I have very strong legs from swimming and jogging all the time. There is a hill on the other side of the pond and running up and down it will help me build endurance for this 90-minute game. It will also help build my abdominal muscles, which provide a center of gravity and help with balance. One must stop and go often in this game, so balance plays a big roll in scoring.

The next day, we met on the soccer field again and BreAnna did some more shopping for gear needed to play the goalie position. She handed Angela a pair of gloves then started telling us how the goalkeeper needed extra protection. She asked Angela to pay close attention to the things that will protect her from injury. BreAnna pulled out a long-sleeved shirt that had padded shoulders and elbows, and a pair of shorts that had extra padding to protect her hips. She explained that to protect the net sometimes you fall on the ground because it is the only way to stop the ball from going in. The latex gloves provide extra grip on the ball when it is kicked high in the air and the pads in the shorts protect you if you fall to the ground while trying to catch the ball.

Angela and Sara took one end of the field and BreAnna and myself took the other end of the field and just had fun kicking and goalkeeping with the ball. After around an hour of getting a feel for the game, we came to a unanimous agreement that we would be good at this game and that playing would be an enjoyable experience.

Next we decided to start the search for the team we were going to join. We spent the next two weekends going to games and looking for the right team for us. We all agreed that the team we were going to join needed to be competitive. Scholarships are given to gifted players for college and you need to be on a good team to get noticed. Word gets out really quick about good players.

Elite teams get the opportunity to travel around the region or even around the country to play other high-level teams for weeklong tournaments. If the team keeps winning, they get to play in a championship game at the end of the tournament. It all sounds so exciting.

We are having a blast practicing and searching for the right team to join. We have our eyes on a team called Spring Tide, which means a great flood or rush of emotions. That's a good description of what this game can do to you. Emotions run higher for the players as well as the fans than they do in any other game known to mankind. There is something about this non-stop game that gets the adrenaline flowing.

We followed the Spring Tide team to their next two games and all four of us agreed that this was the team for us. We approached the coach and he said he wanted to see what we had to offer. His name was Mr. Hicks and he takes coaching very seriously. We wanted to show him our talent by playing each other, like we do when we practice. We had some fancy moves that we thought we could impress him with, but instead he wanted us to go up against his present team members. First he wanted to see the goalkeeping abilities of Angela and BreAnna. Coach Hicks put his best forward on both of them and BreAnna was able to block 5 out of 8 kicks while Angela blocked 4 out of 8. Next, Sara and myself were asked to try to score on the team's best goalkeeper. I was able to make a couple of high kicks past her, but none of my ground balls made it into the goal. However, Sara got a couple on the ground into the net.

Afterwards, we all looked at each other, thinking about how humbling it was to play with all of these excellent soccer players. We didn't think we had much of a chance, but the coach saw that we had potential and asked if we could come to practice the next day. He saw talent in us and we were appreciative.

To celebrate being accepted on the Spring Tide soccer team, I put together a party. School was out for the summer and the family decided to have a stay at home vacation, so spending more time with my friends was on my summer agenda.

The first couple to arrive was BreAnna and Jake and behind them was Zack. Everyone had instructions to come straight to the backyard, through the side gate. Zack had a boom box on his shoulder playing country music. He two-stepped all the way to the picnic table. Then he grabbed me and we finished two-stepping until the song was over. BreAnna and Jake clapped their hands when we were finished.

Zack gave me a bear hug and lifted me off my feet and said, "How's my favorite girl?"

I replied, "Doing just great. I am excited about life again and about being on the Spring Tide soccer team. That sport is a big part of why I am back to myself." BreAnna said, "That's right, we are calling ourselves head bangers because we are so good at hitting the ball with our foreheads. It is a fitting name for us."

Through the gate came Sara and Kyle and right behind them were Angela and Brad.

We all gave each other knuckle bumps and BreAnna said, "Glad to see our other two head bangers could make it here." Everyone got a kick out of that little statement.

Brad pulled off his shirt and said, "Last one to the pond is a rotten egg!" Everyone started pulling off his or her shirts or cover ups and ran to the pond. I was the last one to make it to the pond, so I guess I was the rotten egg, but I didn't want one of my guests to be last. They took turns swinging out on the rope that was tied to the big oak tree and letting go once they were at the middle of the pond. There was a lot of splashing going on. I saw Bam peeking around a bush. She was in one of her shy moods, so I slipped over to where she was hiding and gave her a scratch behind her ear. She nudged me with her nose as if to say thank you.

We were having a blast swimming in the spring-fed pond when my favorite two-stepping song started playing.

I said, "Everyone, out of the pond! Grab your partner and follow me!"

I grabbed Zack and we proceeded to two-step around the pond. When the song ended, Zack continued to hold my hand and we sat on the bench by the pond. Zack said, "It is great to have you back in good spirits. I've missed the fun side of you."

I replied, "It is great to be back. When I was in that haze of sadness I lost control of myself. Soccer has brought me back to reality. When I met Jeff my whole world changed. I had no idea how a crush can change everything about your life. I was completely consumed with just the thought of Jeff. We had only held hands, but he changed my life in the same way BreAnna and Jake's lives were changed when they met. I think maybe I was in love with Jeff. After the accident the feeling I got when holding Jeff's hand was no longer there. It is as if a different person is in his body. I had thoughts of kissing Jeff all the time and how wonderful it would be. Now he doesn't even acknowledge my presence, much less our history together. You know, Zack, I am soon to be seventeen and have yet to be kissed by anyone besides my family, which is only on the forehead or cheek. I just feel so out of touch with what teens are experiencing at my age. Sweet sixteen has not been so sweet for me."

Zack said, "I would kiss you in a second, but I would not risk our relationship over something that might make you feel awkward around me in the future. Friends are polite to each other, but they don't always tell you the truth about how they are feeling. They usually start acting differently and the next thing you know they stop calling or coming by to see you. That's all because they felt awkward because of some silly emotion that turned out not to be shared."

I said, "If you would like to kiss me, I promise not to get all emotional and awkward or to make you embarrassed or uneasy in the future. I will be very adult about the whole thing."

Before I even finished trying to convince Zack that our relationship would never change because of a little old kiss, his eyes were upon my lips and I could feel him moving closer and closer until words were no longer coming out of my mouth. I could feel his breath on my lips and they began to tingle. I was being drawn to his lips as if they were a magnetic field. My limbs were becoming limp and powerless. I was being drawn to his plump lips with such splendor and magnitude that there was no turning back. I'm the aggressor now, moving ever so slowly but with bold assertiveness towards his lips until we connect. What I feel is total bliss and happiness as his lips move against mine. My eyes close without thought to what is happening; I'm melting into Zack's arms.

A big splash in the water brought me back to reality.

Zack looked at me and a smile came across his face. He said, "Are you okay?"

I smiled back and replied, "That was the sweetest thing that has ever happened to me. Yes, I am okay and we are okay. I would like to do that again sometime."

Sara let it be know she was hungry and suggested we all go get some food for our stomachs. Zack put his favorite line dance song on his boom box and we all line danced to the picnic table. I went in the house to get bread, meat and cheese to make sandwiches with. The tea was already in a container with ice for everyone to pour, as they needed it. We really worked up an appetite from swimming in the pond. When you really are hungry, food tastes so good.

After we filled our tummies, I announced that we would be drawing straws and the short straw would share a long word that would be helpful in our vocabulary to express ourselves in a way that had an intelligent ring to it. The one to come up with the short straw was Jake. The word he chose was proprietary, which means being owned by a private individual or corporation under a trademark or patent. You see, Jake the genius is filing for a patent on an invention he came up with to control unwanted noise. It is a filter that fits over windows for people who live close to trains or who live in big cities that never sleep. Sound will just bounce off the window if treated with this technology.

The second time we draw straws is for some advice that will help us live for 100 years. Angela drew the short straw this time. Her advice was not to carry mental baggage around. If you have hurt someone, ask for their forgiveness and if someone hurt you, let them know and then throw the hurt away. Mental strains take years off your life and they lead to an addiction of numbing the brain.

I'm proud of my friends for sharing things that will make life better for all of us in the long run. Jeff shared this great gift with me and now I am sharing it with my friends. I will email him the results tonight, however he will not have a clue as to what I am talking about.

We have had enough sit down time and now it is time to show the guys what we have learned in practice about soccer.

BreAnna started off with, "Coach Hicks saw that all four of us girls had potential to make good soccer players because of our physical attributes such as strength in our legs, speed that surpasses some of the other current players, and stamina which is required to play such a long game. He said we lack knowledge of the game but he will teach us what we need to know. Once we learn all the tactical moves, we will be depending more on our teammates than on Coach Hicks. To become a winning team all 11 players must bond and become team players. There is no 'I' in 'team'.

Once on the field, the team will have three or four defenders, two or three forwards, which is the perfect position for Chelsea, and five mid-fielders, which Sara is perfect for. Angela and myself make good goalkeepers because we are so tall and are able to block high with our hands and low with our legs.

Field players can cover as much as five miles during a game, so if you think Sara is skinny now just what will she look like when summer is over! Chelsea is the best head banger Coach Hicks has ever seen. She made two goals on me before I even knew what was happening. Each goal counts as one point, and the most goals wins the match. The clock stops only after a goal is scored or on a penalty kick or if the referee specifically calls for it. You play for 45 minutes with a 15-minute halftime. This is really the only time the coach has to talk to you about strategy. An outsider can see things that players sometimes miss.

The end boundaries of the field are called the goal lines and the side boundaries are called touchlines. The center of the field, called the center circle, has a radius of 10 yards that surround the center spot. The ball is out of play when it crosses the touchline or the goal line. The referee drops the ball between the opposing teams to restart the game, and the ball must have contact with the ground before players can kick the ball. The girls would like to give a demonstration of what we have learned about this game if you guys would like to see."

That's all it took and the guys were clapping their hands saying, "Bring it on!" I used cornmeal to mark the goal line and we used the wooden fence for the net. BreAnna was first to guard the goal and I showed off my head-banging move to make the first goal. I take the ball between my feet to manipulate it where my knee can bounce it high enough for my forehead to bang it above BreAnna's arms. Everyone went wild when I scored the first point.

Next, Sara began kicking the ball but was unable to score on BreAnna. She tried kicking the ball 10 times, but BreAnna was on top of things. Angela traded places with BreAnna and caught the ball with her hands when I tried a sidekick. Then Sara kicked the ball on the ground and scored a point on Angela, and once again the guys went nuts.

Brad was getting edgy; you could see his nervous tension from not being able to play until he suddenly burst out saying, "How about BreAnna, Chelsea and Sara all play defenders and Angela plays goalkeeper against one of us guys at a time. It will be good practice for the girls and the guys won't be so bored."

Everyone was in agreement and Brad was first to take on the girls. As defenders of the goal, also sometimes called fullbacks, our job is to keep the ball away from the goal area. Strong legs are a plus for this position and BreAnna is the strongest of the girls so she will play closest to the goal line. The rest of us will be in front, face to face with Brad. Eye contact was Brad's strongest point. He kept his foot on the ball and his eyes on us. He somehow missed his first try even though he got past all of the defenders. Angela was able to block the ball that never left the ground. Next Brad tried an air ball and BreAnna blocked it.

Brad said, "I think I am starting to get the feel for the ball now, so you girls had better watch out!"

Angela said, "Bring it on, big boy, we are ready for you!"

About that time, Brad kicked the ball right past all four of us. It was so fast we didn't have time to react. I think Brad broke our concentration and that was his tactic to score on us. We better be aware of Brad.

Next to challenge our abilities to keep the ball out of the goal area is Jake. He is using his calculating ability to find our weak link. He is kicking the ball around letting us return it without really trying to get it in the goal. We all sense his scheming ways to get the ball past us. Suddenly the ball is airborne and is too high for Angela to catch with her hands. Jake threw his arm in the air as if to proclaim victory and runs back to the picnic table demanding high fives from the rest of the guys.

BreAnna said, "Don't be in such a big hurry to celebrate. The ball was too high and would have gone over the goal netting. That means is doesn't count." The guys dismissed what BreAnna said and next on the field was Kyle.

The ball was kicked in my direction and I caught it right on the flat part of my forehead to block Kyle's goal.

Kyle said, "That's amazing, I now see why you call yourselves the head bangers." Everyone got a chuckle out of that.

He kicked the ball towards Sara next and she repeated what I had just done. Next Angela hit the ball with her head and Kyle said, "I surrender! You head bangers are the best."

Next on the field came Zack. The ball immediately flies past all the defenders but Angela leaps into the air and catches the ball. Next Zack tries a fake to the left, but with four defenders lined up, he doesn't make it past the line. He's been on the field for nearly ten minutes and is determined to score. Four against one may seem unfair but those guys asked for it so there is no taking pity on them. Zack looked like he was going to fake again and we all headed for the left side of the field, but he kicked it right instead and made a goal. Immediately his arms went into the air for a victory cheer as he exited the field. High fives were in order from all the guys.

If I may say so myself, Zack did earn his moment of glory, after all it took him 15 minutes to score. He was persistent about getting a goal. Males have this companionship thing about them that makes them always cheer each other on. We have no intention of trying to steal their moment of manhood.

So we just said, "Nice game."

The party came to an end and everyone had a great time. When the last car pulled out of the driveway, I walked to the pear tree that Matt helped me plant, and said to it, "Jeff would be proud of this day, if only he could remember the things he taught me."

I felt silly talking to a tree but at the same time it was symbolic of the wonderful days on that Florida beach where I met Jeff. I reminisced on the bygone experiences of when Jeff told the story about the pear tree he planted to provide extra potassium for his muscles. Then that awful accident with the faulty football helmet happened. People think their plans in life will work out if they do the right thing, but you really don't have a clue how they will turn out. You must live life with faith. You have to accept certain things that you have no control over.

That evening, I contacted Jeff's mother to see if Jeff felt like talking. I always contact his mother and she sits in front of the computer with Jeff for support. He has no idea who this crazy girl is that always wants to talk to him, nevertheless, I continue to try and jog his memory. He is always polite but the distance between us is always there. I told him about Jake choosing the word proprietary as our new big word to add to our vocabulary, and Angela who gave advice to not carry mental baggage around and he just looked at me like, who are you, without understanding what I was talking about.

Then Jeff's mothers added to the conversation, "Jeff learned to tie his shoe strings all by himself today." This brought me back to the reality of his situation. Jeff's mind is still not there due to the accident. I continued to talk to Jeff anyways, hoping that somehow I will help him on his journey in life. We said our goodbyes, and I turned off the computer.

The diving lessons were paying off as we all dove into Lake Tenkiller with the diving team. As we went deeper and deeper the fish got bigger and bigger. I reached out to touch a very large catfish and thoughts went through my mind about how Zack catches catfish by putting his hand in their mouths and dragging them to shore. I think just touching the fins is enough for me. My mom swam next to me and gave me thumbs up to let me know she is having a good time. Dad was on the other side of the fish and stroked its head, which by the way was bigger than my head. The fish was also longer than my body. It was huge. The deeper we went, the colder and darker it became. We all have underwater flashlights though, so that we won't get lost.

At the very bottom of the lake are some white fish. I have never seen completely white fish before and everyone's flashlights were on them. There must have been twenty of them. They have an elongated body with a long snout and teeth overlapping as if they were snarling at us. I am glad right now that I have a heavy waterproof diving suit on. It's my armor of protection from these monsters.

Our instructor was heading to the surface and I was right behind him. Bubbles were all around us from the other divers and it was a sight to see. Dad was the last to surface and he had a turtle in his hand. The propeller of a boat must have hit it at some time because it only had three legs. One of its hind legs was missing. That must be why Dad was able to catch him. Since I was already on the boat, Dad handed the turtle to me. He was very small but full on energy. His three legs and his head were going in every direction, like he was still swimming. We passed him around for everyone to see the catch of the day and then turned him loose to swim away.

We all had a great time and exchanged stories about what all each of us had seen while under the water. We all agreed that the white fish at the bottom of the lake was the most exciting thing to see and the cool darkness was the most dramatic sensation of the day. Only our instructor had gone that deep before. All and all it was a great experience.

The first soccer game for us to play with Spring Tide begins in two hours. We are all super excited. BreAnna had all of us meet at her house to warm up before we hit the field. We did a lot of stretching and some yoga moves that will help us focus. BreAnna demanded our undivided attention to go over some of our weak points. She said, "We must stay focused and not allow distractions to interfere with our talent. Brad never would have scored on us if we hadn't allowed him to distract us with his talk. We must keep our eyes on the ball at all times and stay in position on the field. In order to beat them we must be aware of where they are at all times. Know your enemy."

We loaded up in BreAnna's car and she was still giving pointers during the drive to the game. She talked about how Coach Hicks plays everybody on the team. You will play either on the first half of the game or the second half. The coach agreed to let the four head bangers play the first half of the game. Your first impression is important and there could be some scouts in the stands.

It is a beautiful summer day with a light breeze to keep things cool. The stands are beginning to fill and our opponents just now entered the field. Their uniforms are blue and white striped and the name of the team is Hurricane Force. They are from Florida and are undefeated. The Spring Tide lost a game to them earlier in the season but the score was close. Our uniform colors are red and white stripes and we all wear a rubber bracelet that says, "We are driven." It is a reminder of what got the team to this point.

Coach Hicks placed BreAnna as goalkeeper, myself as head banging forward and Angela and Sara as defenders because of their strong legs. Right before the game began, Angela pointed towards the bleachers, climbing the stairs was Brad, Zack, Kyle, and Jake, in that order.

BreAnna said, "Girls, I know it is exciting that the guys came to watch us, but we must stay focused. Let their presence be an inspiration to you, but not a distraction." With that we marched onto the field and took our positions.

BreAnna made pasta with tomato sauce to energize us, and now I'm feeling the effects. Coach Hicks recommended we eat two hours before the game. BreAnna took the instructions very seriously.

Before we knew it, the game had started and the ball was under my foot. The coaches words were ringing in my ears, "Relax your body when you have the ball, this is the secret to total control of the ball. Tense players always get the ball stolen right out from under their foot."

I began dribbling the ball keeping it close to my feet with small quick kicks. I'm totally aware of my surroundings and so into the moment. The Hurricane Force team is very aggressive and I felt contact from every direction, yet I am so relaxed that at this moment nothing can keep me from making a goal. I scored easily, and my arms went into the air and I began turning in circles with electric intensity of which I have never experienced. My sharp shooting skills are shining as bright as the sun itself.

I can hear Zack hollering, "You go, Chelsea! That's

my favorite girl!"

I have always believed that athletic, physically strong players are at their best when everything is right in their lives. Now this theory has been put to the test and is a fact as far as I'm concerned. I have willingly accepted the fact that Jeff has no idea who I am and may even think I am stalking him, which is very gross to me, and he very well may never recall what we had. I'm finally able to put this chapter of my life on hold for now. Soccer snapped me out of the haze that dominated my life for the past year. I'm back and it is showing up in this game. Soccer has lifted the dark cloud and now the sun is shining on my face. My new motto is, that was then and this is now.

The great thing about soccer is that anyone who has possession of the ball can score no matter what position he or she plays. If the opportunity is there, you can take a shot.

The ball is in play once again and the Hurricane Force has kicked the ball. Because the initial kicker is not permitted to play the ball a second time until another player touches it, Angela was able to gain control of the ball and once again we are heading in the direction of our goal. Angela kicked the ball in the air and one of the Spring Tide midfielders hit the ball with their hand to guide it into the net. This was a big mistake because only the goalkeeper is allowed to use their hands. Once again the Hurricane Force has the ball.

The ball is moving down the field rapidly when one of the Spring Tide players blocked the ball temporarily. The Hurricane Force quickly regained control. I saw a player plant her non-kicking foot a little way from the ball and swing her kicking leg back to strike the bottom of the ball with her shoe laces and follow through to make a long lofted kick only to wind up in BreAnna's hands. The crowd went nuts.

Spring Tide once again has control of the ball and a player kicked it in my direction and I made a heading move with my forehead and put the ball in Angela's direction. The ball was a little too high for Angela to use her leg and too low to control with her chest so she used her thigh. This is the first time I have seen this move. The ball is still heading in the direction of our goal and is on the ground now. As we approach our goal to score, the ball stays on the ground and is kicked past two defenders only to be stopped by the goalkeeper who fell to the ground to stop the ball with her body. The crowd is now on their feet and they are so loud it is impossible to hear my teammates.

The intensity of the game continued until half time and the score remained one to zero. It is time for a drink of water. My body is drenched in sweat. High fives were coming at me in every direction. I had scored the only goal so far and all of the attention was on me. I put a towel on my head to calm myself from all the excitement. Coach Hicks peeks under my towel to tell me, 'good job'.

The second half of the game was just as fierce but the Hurricane Force managed to score two goals for a final score of two to one.

On our way back to BreAnna's house, the mood was joyous. Even though we had lost the game, the head bangers scored the only point for our team and the Hurricane Force could not score against the head bangers. BreAnna saw the game as a victory.

She said, "Maybe if we had invited the whole team over for pasta with tomato sauce, we would have won the game." BreAnna always had a way of sprinkling her version of teamwork around so everyone benefits.

Who would have thought that some Johnny come lately could have done such a good job as we did? Now that we have the Spring Tide's respect, we can be more vocal with our strategy and they will listen. Summer is winding down and I am happy and once again enjoying life to the fullest. Life is a bed of roses; sometimes you get stuck by one of its thorns. The sweet smell of the roses always makes the pain worth it though.

Jeff asked if I would stop calling him until he could remember who I was. It was good that he made that request, because it allowed me to move on with my life. Jeff's mother called the other day to let me know that Jeff was humming the song I had always played for him over the phone. That was nice to hear. Jeff will always have a place in my heart, even when I'm a centenarian, and I will always remember the feeling I had when I had touched his hand. The strength of his spirit lives inside me, for the measure of a man is how he lives.

He always said, "Doing the right thing just feels right. You have to live with every decision you make in life, so take it easy on yourself, and do the right thing." I'm sure he hasn't a clue he ever said such a thing, but by setting me free like he did, I know that Jeff is somewhere in that body.

The End

References:

1)   *Riverside Webster's II New College Dictionary*
2)   *Holy Bible*